ULTIMA...

BUYERS' GUIDE

Lotus Elise

In all its forms
(including Exige and Europa)

Johnny Tipler
PMM Books

Copyright: Johnny Tipler, 2011

Photo credits: Lotus Cars, Jason Parnell, Antony Fraser, Wim te Riet, Johnny Tipler
Edited by Peter Morgan
Design and layout by SD Design, www.dorringtondesign.co.uk
Printed and bound in India by Replika Press Pvt. Ltd.

First published 2011

ISBN 978 1 906712 09 9

Published by PMM Books, an imprint of Peter Morgan Media Ltd.
PO Box 2561, Marlborough, Wiltshire, SN8 1YD, Great Britain.
Telephone: +44 1672 514038
E-mail: sales@pmmbooks.com
Website: www.pmmbooks.com

Contents

The Lotus Elise was launched at the Frankfurt Show in 1995 and, typical of model evolutions, that car became known retrospectively as the Series 1 when its successor arrived five years later. The Elise was named after the granddaughter of the firm's then owner, Romano Artioli, whose Christian name conveniently began with the letter 'E' like most Lotus models, from Elite to Esprit, and now the Evora. Designed and built within two fraught years the Elise embodied the core values laid down three decades earlier by Lotus founder Colin Chapman: high performance through light weight, race-derived suspension, and efficient though not overlarge powertrains, all clad in aerodynamic, lightweight fibreglass bodywork.

To buy an Elise is to buy into those principals, and by association, into 60 years of Lotus history. And what a history, for the company can boast seven F1 World Championships, 79 Grand Prix victories and innumerable race wins in the 1960s and '70s, when to be a successful racing driver was synonymous with driving a Lotus. Though a spent force in F1 by the end of the 1980s, the marque survived as a road car producer after Chapman's death in 1982 under the umbrella of General Motors. Lotus was later taken over by Bugatti owner Snr Artioli, who had the majority share from 1993 to 1996, before he sold out to Proton to pay his Bugatti debts.

The Elise survived the departure of Snr Artioli and flourished under new owners, Malaysian car manufacturer Proton, although it was actually sister company Lotus Engineering's pioneering consultancy work honing and fine-tuning products for other car makers worldwide that proved to be the most profitable part of the business. It was this depth of in-house expertise as much as the efficiency and adaptability of a small volume production operation that allowed the Elise's gestation to come to fruition so quickly.

With its unique construction built around a super-strong extruded aluminium chassis and clothed in delectably curvaceous panelwork, this was no mainstream sportscar model of the sort exemplified by the Mazda MX5/Miata. Always a radical proposition, 15 years down the line the Elise is a proven concept, confident that anything its peers can do, it can match, and more. Precise, flamboyant and passionately extrovert, the pocket rocket out-handles any exotic supercar on a twisty road, and in its supercharged format, outperforms most of them too.

There are some fundamental questions to ask when seeking out an Elise.

First things first: how much can you afford to spend? On a tight budget, it has to be a basic Series 1. Money no object? You're in the happy hunting ground of the supercharged Series 2 SC.

Is it looks that count? If you're taken with the purer, rounded contours, ovoid headlight nacelles and air scoops of the original car you'll have to stick to Series 1s, though late '90s cars will allow you to access quicker and slightly dearer versions such as the 111S.

And what about build quality? In 2000 the Series 2 Elise ushered in much improved build quality, which had been insisted upon by its General Motors clients when Lotus undertook construction of the Elise-based Vauxhall/Opel/Daewoo VX220 Roadster. But if it's to be your second car, and you prefer the aesthetics of the Series 1, the superior

Lotus Elises, Exiges & 2-Eleven at LOG 28, Snowmass, Colorado, 2007

build quality of the Series 2 may not be a clincher.

Need more attitude? Shop for an Exige, though again you have to decide whether you prefer the original rounded Series 1 version or the better-built Series 2.

Is it creature comforts that matter? That brings us to the unsung hero of the Elise line-up, the Europa. It's built on the Elise chassis, finished inside more like a grand tourer and powered by the VX220's 2.0-litre GM turbo engine – a very nice and rather underrated package.

Once you've answered these questions to your satisfaction, you might still be turned off by a particular car. If it's not a colour you like

or a specification you want, it's a straightforward reject. Secondly, there may be issues about crash damage in its history file. Thirdly, a lack of sustained and documented service history could put you off, and fourthly, a suspiciously large number of owners might suggest a rogue car.

If you are considering purchasing an Elise you are very lucky indeed and I hope this glovebox-sized guide will prove indispensible in choosing the right model for you.

This Ultimate Buyers' Guide includes all the important core information on the Lotus Elise. The after-sales support and service network for Lotus owners is well-established. There are many excellent sources of advice and

Lotus unveiled projected Elise for 2015 at Paris Salon 2010

support and an established network of experienced specialists.

Expert advice is best sought at an early stage in your quest from the cross section of owners and specialists who look after Elise models on a daily basis. I talked extensively with two such authorities in the course of my research: Guy Munday of Stratton Motor Company, and Greg Lock of Hangar 111, who we'll meet later on.

Our first port of call in the quest for enlightenment is the Stratton Motor Company at Long Stratton, a small town straddling the A140 Ipswich road in south Norfolk, less than half-an-hour from the Hethel plant where the cars are made. The busy late-night petrol station fronts a big showroom displaying Lotuses and Morgans, while Astons lurk in an enclave beside the indoor display. There's always a cross section of modern Lotuses and the occasional classic on offer. A dedicated aficionado, Guy frequently commentates at Lotus Cars' anniversary events as well as club functions, and he enjoys sharing his passion with fellow devotees and aspiring owners. We'll hear his opinions as we home in on the specific models.

Johnny Tipler,
Norwich, England

1994

Elise 'step-in car' concept begins to gel. First sketches, renderings and clay bucks.

1995

Prototype Elise M1-11 in testing at venues like Nardò in southern Italy and the Stelvio pass in the Italian Alpine foothills.
Elise debuts at Frankfurt Show.

1996

Malaysian HiCom Group's Proton subsidiary acquires major stake in Group Lotus.

1997

Lotus Elise Trophy introduced in Italy, staged by Peroni Promotions. Sport Elise Sprint 190 announced in March. Elise-based GT1 racecars in action in FIA GT Championship. Lotus Cars matches international quality control standard ISO QS 9000. Water-based paint first trialled. May sees 1,000th Elise built

1998

Proton ups its holding to control 80% of Group Lotus. From initial output of 750 vehicles, annual Elise production is now running at 3,300 units. September sees Lotus's 50th anniversary celebrations; half the 1,500 Lotuses in attendance are Elises. Sport 135 model introduced.

1999

143bhp/105kW Elise 111S with developed VVC K-series engine announced at Geneva. Minimalist 340R concept car launched (340 units made). Motorsport Elise unveiled at Earls Court

2000

Lotus builds GM's VX220 Speedster. In May the Sport 160 and Sport 190 are introduced. 177bhp/130kW (192bhp/140kW in track-spec) Exige S1 launched. In October the Series 2 Elise is announced, still using Rover K-series powertrain.

2001

Upgraded 135R version available.

2004

Series 2 Exige on sale. Federal Elise on sale in USA. 189bhp/139kW 111R available in Europe and rest of world. Toyota ZZ 1.8-litre twin-cam engine and 6-speed gearbox replace K-series driveline.

2005

243bhp/178kW supercharged Sport Exige R released at Geneva in March (50 units built). Elise 111R and Sport Racer models shown. Limited run (50 cars) Lotus Elise Sport on sale.

2006

Exige S and Europa 2.0 launched at Geneva. Tesla Roadster electric prototype unveiled, built on Elise chassis. ProBax seats, LED tail-lights and ECUs introduced. Lotus decals on rear changed to embossed lettering. North American Exige on sale in USA, 220bhp/161kW supercharged Exige S unleashed.

2007

Federally correct lights and bumpers fitted, having been exempt for 3 years. Elise S released and 111R renamed Elise R. Spec includes airbags, ABS brakes, electric windows and carpet.

2008

Elise 270E ethanol-fuelled model up and running. Main models are 134bhp/98kW, 5-speed Elise S, 189bhp/139kW 6-speed Elise R and 218bhp/160kW 6-speed, supercharged Elise SC. Exige S 240 available with 240bhp/176kW.

2009

Exige S 260 released. Stealth black Exige Scura launched. Highly tuned Exige GT3 available for competition.

2010

Base model Elise S and Exige offer 9-percent reduction in CO_2 and better fuel-economy, with combined figure of 37.2mls/gall (7.6l/100km or 31mls/USg). Elise R and Elise SC return 29mls/gall (9.7l/100km or 24mls/USg) and 28mls/gall (10l/100km or 23mls/USg) respectively.

2011

Fresh styling cues, new front clam featuring almond-eye headlights, Evora-like mouth and air intakes; revised rear bumper and engine cover; all-in-one integrated headlights including LED daylight running lights and LED direction indicators; better aerodynamics with 4-percent reduction in drag coefficient. Entry-level 134bhp 1600cc Toyota 1ZR-FAE engine introduced.

Elise Matrix	Elise S1 (1996)	Elise 135 Sport (1998)	Elise 111S (1999)
ENGINE			
Number of cylinders	4	4	4
Displacement	1796	1796	1796
Engine layout/ Drive	Mid engine	Mid engine	Mid engine
Max. Power			
UK Horse Power (HP)	118	135	143
PS	120	137	145
Kilowatts	87	100	105
Max. torque			
lb-ft	122	121	128
Nm	165	164	174
Engine Model	K-series	K-series	K-series VVC
Induction Method	Naturally Aspirated	Naturally Aspirated	Naturally Aspirated
Transmission	5-speed Manual	5-speed Manual	5-speed Manual
PERFORMANCE			
Top speed (mph/kph)	126/202	128/205	135/216
Acceleration from 0 - 60 mph (sec)	5.7	5	5.3
Acceleration from 0 - 100 kph (0 - 62 mph, sec)	5.9	N/a	N/a
Acceleration from 0 - 100 mph (160kph, sec)	18	N/a	14.4
FUEL CONSUMPTION			
Urban (mls/UK gall, l/100km, mls/US gall)	28.9, 9.6, 24		
Combined	39.4, 7.1, 32.8	30, 9.4, 25	30.7, 9.2, 25.6
Extra urban	49.9, 5.7, 41.6		
BODY			
Length, mm (ins)	3726 (146.7ins)	3726 (146.7ins)	3726 (146.7ins)
Width, mm (ins)	1701 (67ins)	1701 (67ins)	1701 (67ins)
Height, mm (ins)	1202 (47.3ins)	1202 (47.3ins)	1202 (47.3ins)
Wheelbase, mm (ins)	2300 (90.6ins)	2300 (90.6ins)	2300 (90.6ins)
Unladen Lightest weight (curb) kg/lb	725/1598	730/1609	770/1698
WHEELS			
Front	5-spoke alloy 5.5Jx15	5-spoke alloy 5.5Jx15	5-spoke alloy 5.5Jx15
Rear	5-spoke alloy 7Jx16	5-spoke alloy 7Jx16	5-spoke alloy 7Jx16
TYRES			
Front, Make	Pirelli P Zero	Pirelli P Zero	Pirelli P Zero
Front, Size	185/55 R15	185/55 R15	185/55 R15
Rear, Make	Pirelli P Zero	Pirelli P Zero	Pirelli P Zero
Rear, Size	205/50 R16	205/45 R16	225/45 R16
GEAR RATIOS			
First	3.167	2.923	2.923
Second	1.842	1.75	1.75
Third	1.308	1.308	1.308
Fourth	1.033	1.033	1.033
Fifth	0.765	0.848	0.848
Sixth	None	None	None
Reverse	3.00	3.00	3.00

Elise Sport 160 (2000)	Elise Sport 190 (2001)	Elise S2 (2001)	Elise S2 135R (2001)	Elise S2 111S (2002)
4	4	4	4	4
1796	1796	1796	1796	1796
Mid engine	Mid engine	Mid engine	Mid engine	Mid engine
157	190	120	135	156
159	193	122	137	158
117	142	90	100	116
128	139	124	124	129
174	189	168	168	175
K-series	K-series VHPD	K-series	K-series	K-series
Naturally Aspirated	Naturally Aspirated	Naturally Aspirated	Naturally Aspirated	Naturally Aspirated
5-speed Manual	5-speed Manual	5-speed Manual	5-speed Manual	5-speed Manual
130/208	135/216	125/200	127/204	128/205
5	4.3	5.6	5.4	5
N/a	4.4	N/a	5.5	N/a
N/a	10.7	18.2	15	14
N/a	N/a	27.4, 10.3, 22.9	N/a	30, 9.4, 25
3726 (146.7ins)	3726 (146.7ins)	3785 (149ins)	3785 (149ins)	3785 (149ins)
1701 (67ins)	1701 (67ins)	1719 (67.7ins)	1719 (67.7ins)	1719 (67.7ins)
1202 (47.3ins)	1202 (47.3ins)	1117 (44.0ins)	1117 (44.0ins)	1117 (44.0ins)
2300 (90.6ins)	2300 (90.6ins)	2300 (90.6ins)	2300 (90.6ins)	2300 (90.6ins)
715/1576	670/1477	750/1654	750/1654	780/1720
5-spoke alloy 5.5Jx15	5-spoke alloy 5.5Jx15	6-spoke alloy	6-spoke alloy	8 spoke alloys 5.5 x 16
5-spoke alloy 7Jx16	5-spoke alloy 7Jx16	6-spoke alloy	6-spoke alloy	8 spoke alloy 7.5 x 17
Pirelli P Zero	Pirelli P Zero	Yokohama Neova AD07	Yokohama Neova AD07	Yokohama Neova AD07
185/55 R15	185/55 R15	175/55R16	195/50R16	195/50R16
Pirelli P Zero	Pirelli P Zero	Yokohama Neova AD07	Yokohama Neova AD07	Yokohama Neova AD07
225/45 R16	225/45 R16	225/45R17	225/45R17	225/45R17
2.923	2.923	N/a	N/a	N/a
1.75	1.75			
1.308	1.308			
1.033	1.033			
0.848	0.848			
None	None			
3.00	3.00			

Elise Matrix *continued...*	Elise S2 R (2004)	Elise S2 S (2006)	Elise S2 SC (2007)
ENGINE			
Number of cylinders	4	4	4
Displacement	1796 cm3	1794 cm3	1796 cm3
Engine layout/ Drive	Mid engine	Mid engine	Mid engine
Max. Power			
UK Horse Power (HP)	189 hp @ 7800 rpm	134 hp @ 6200 rpm	217 hp @ 8000 rpm
PS	192 PS @ 7800 rpm	136 PS @ 6200 rpm	220 PS @ 8000 rpm
Kilowatts	141 kW @ 7800 rpm	100 kW @ 6200 rpm	162 kW @ 8000 rpm
Max. torque			
lb-ft	133 lb.ft @ 6800 rpm	127 lb.ft @ 4200 rpm	154.8 lb.ft @ 5000 rpm
Nm	181 Nm @ 6800 rpm	172 Nm @ 4200 rpm	210 Nm @ 5000 rpm
Engine Model	Toyota 2ZZ	Toyota 1ZZ	Toyota 2ZZ
Induction Method	Naturally Aspirated	Naturally Aspirated	Supercharged
Transmission	6-speed Manual	5-speed Manual	6-speed Manual
PERFORMANCE			
Top speed (mph/kph)	138/222	129/208	145/233
Acceleration from 0 - 60 mph (sec)	5.09	5.72	4.29
Acceleration from 0 - 100 kph (0 - 62 mph, sec)	5.37	6.1	4.6
Acceleration from 0 - 100 mph (160kph, sec)	13.39	16.2	10.77
FUEL CONSUMPTION			
Urban (mls/UK gall, l/100km, mls/US gall)	24.4, 11.6, 20.3	26.7, 10.6, 22.2	23.9, 11.8, 20.0
Combined	34.5, 8.2, 28.7	37.1, 7.6, 31.0	33.2, 8.5, 27.7
Extra urban	45.6, 6.2, 38.0	48.7, 5.8, 40.6	44.1, 6.4, 36.8
BODY			
Length, mm (ins)	3785 (149ins)	3785 (149ins)	3785 (149ins)
Width, mm (ins)	1719 (67.7ins)	1719 (67.7ins)	1719 (67.7ins)
Height, mm (ins)	1117 (44.0ins)	1117 (44.0ins)	1117 (44.0ins)
Wheelbase, mm (ins)	2300 (90.6ins)	2300 (90.6ins)	2300 (90.6ins)
Unladen Lightest weight (curb) kg/lb	860/1896	850/1874	870/1918
WHEELS			
Front	8 spoke alloys 5.5 x 16	6 spoke alloy 5.5 x 16	12 spoke alloy 6.0 x 16
Rear	8 spoke alloy 7.5 x 17	6 spoke alloy 7.5 x 17	12 spoke alloy 8 x 17
TYRES			
Front, Make	Yokohama Neova AD07	Yokohama Neova AD07	Yokohama Neova AD07
Front, Size	175/55 R16	175/55 R16	175/55 R16
Rear, Make	Yokohama Neova AD07	Yokohama Neova AD07	Yokohama Neova AD07
Rear, Size	225/45 R17	225/45 R17	225/45 R17
GEAR RATIOS			
First	3.116	3.166 :1	3.116
Second	2.05	1.904 :1	2.05
Third	1.481	1.392 :1	1.481
Fourth	1.166	1.031 :1	1.166
Fifth	0.916	0.815 :1	0.916
Sixth	0.815	N/A	0.815
Reverse	3.25	3.250 :1	3.25
Final drive	4.529	4.312 :1	4.529

Elise S2 (2010)
4
1598cm3
Mid engine
134 hp @ 6800 rpm
136 PS @ 6800 rpm
100 kW @ 6800 rpm
118 lb.ft @ 4400 rpm
160 Nm @ 4400 rpm
Toyota 1ZR
Naturally Aspirated
6-speed Manual
127/204
6.01
6.55
18.63
34, 8.31, 28.3
45.0, 6.28, 37.5
56.0, 5.04, 46.7
3785 (149ins)
1719 (67.7ins)
1117 (44.0ins)
2300 (90.6ins)
857/1889
12 spoke alloy 5.5 x 16
12 spoke alloy 7.5 x 17
Yokohama Neova AD07
175/55 R16
Yokohama Neova AD07
225/45 R17
3.538:1
1.913 :1
1.310 :1
0.971 :1
0.818 :1
0.700:1
3.333 :1
4.294 :1

Common data

CHASSIS

Lotus-designed structure of epoxy-bonded sections of aluminium alloy extrusions incorporating roll-over hoop. Fabricated steel rear subframe.

BODY

Composite body panels with detachable front and rear 'clamshells'; integral fixed headlamps. Fuel tank capacity is 40 litres/8.8 UK gallons/10.6 US gallons.

INSTRUMENTATION

Analogue electronic unit comprising speedometer and tachometer with multi-function LCD readout incorporating fuel and coolant gauges, supplied by Stack Instruments.

SUSPENSION

Fully independent with double wishbones with single coil springs over Bilstein monotube dampers all round and Eibach springs. Lotus-patented uprights of extruded aluminium, made by Alusuisse. (Faster models use different spring/ dampers set-ups).

STEERING

Manual rack and pinion steering with 2.8 turns lock-to-lock.

BRAKES

Non-servo split hydraulic system supplied by Automotive Products. Originally 282 mm (11.1ins) diameter aluminium/metal matrix ventilated discs (rotors) made by Lanxide Brembo, replaced by 288mm (11.3ins) cast iron discs: mounted outboard.
S2 has Lotus/AP Racing 2-piston front calipers and Brembo single piston sliding rear calipers with cross-drilled discs (rotors) all round.

DIMENSIONS & CAPACITIES *(if not shown in table)*

Ground clearance	160mm (6.3ins)
Fuel tank capacity	40 litres (8.8 imperial gallons/10.6 US gallons)
Fuel grade	95 RON minimum
Unladen weight	675kg (1,485lb)
Weight distribution	39/61 (% front/rear)
Tyre pressures,cold (S1)	Front: 1.6bar (23psi); Rear: 1.9bar (28psi)
Servicing	First service 1,000 miles (1600km), thereafter every 9,000 miles (15000km) or annually.

Elise Series 1

The original Series 1 Elise was an affordable, individualistic sports car, ideal for the enthusiast who was not overly concerned with creature comforts and appreciated the finer points of the driving experience. It was the only model available until the Sport 135 came out late in 1998.

The Series 1 was styled by Julian Thomson, then Head of Design at Lotus and now Chief Designer at Jaguar. The chassis was designed by Richard Rackham, Lotus's then Chief Engineer and now its Chief Vehicle Architect. Thomson was influenced by a number of automotive icons from the 1960s including the Ferrari 330P4 Le Mans car and its little sister the 246 Dino, as well as Lotus's own Type 23, though he also cited the Ford GT40 and Lancia Stratos as significant. My own favourite parallel is the Ginetta G12, a

mid-engined mid-'60s racer. For his part, chassis man Rackham named the Ducati 916 motorcycle as a principal influence on the Elise design. No surprise there, since supersports bikes are at the cutting edge of design technology.

In accordance with founder Colin Chapman's maxim 'add lightness', Lotus has tended to use lightweight materials and construction rather than brute power to optimise performance and the Elise conforms to type. The Series 1 Lotus Elise weighs only 675kg (1,485 lb), compared for instance to a Porsche Boxster at 1,250 kg (2,756 lb), 74% heavier. It accelerates from 0-60 mph in 5.8 seconds despite its relatively modest power output of 118bhp/87kW from the standard Rover 1.8 L K-series straight-four unit. Braking, cornering, and fuel consumption are

The straightforward but elegant lines of the Elise S1 were drawn by Julian Thomson

The Elise S1 is little more than half the weight of a Porsche Boxster

The body 'clamshells' are made by SOTIRA - and here are in the Hethel paintshop

also improved by the car's low weight. This was a revolutionary car: no one had ever done an extruded aluminium chassis with bonded joints before and then clad it in lightweight fibreglass panels. When Richard Rackham designed the chassis there was no industry standard for bonding aluminium; the new process was developed in-house by Lotus technicians in association with Hydro Aluminium in Denmark, a company subsequently bought by Lotus and now operating as Lotus Lightweight Structures in Worcester. Built on site at Hethel in a long-standing factory building, the Series 1 clamshells and body panels were made using the traditional hand-laid matting/ resin/mould methods which are still deployed on site for lower volume Exige, Europa and circuit racing cars.

From a specification point of view the Series 1 is easy to quantify and categorise because by definition light weight equals few frills. There were only five main options, metallic paint, leather seats, a Category 1 alarm, auxiliary driving lamps and radio fitting kit, and that was it. When they were in current production, an Elise Series 1 with four out of five of those items was considered more desirable, while a cloth interior and no driving lamps was seen as a basic car.

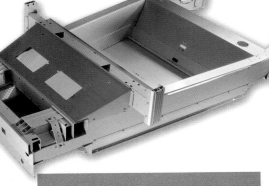

The Elise's simple, but effective aluminium chassis laid bare

HIGH PERFORMANCE VERSIONS
ELISE 111S

A faster edition called the 111S, named after the Lotus type-number of the Elise M111, was introduced in early 1999 and had a VVC Rover K-Series engine with a modified head and VVT variable valve timing technology, producing 143bhp/105kW, along with a closer ratio manual gearbox and lower ratio final drive. The 111S had headlamp covers, rear spoiler, cross-drilled brake discs, alloy window winders and a 6-spoke road wheel design, plus a touch of comfort; extra padding in the seats.

With more power for less money - the 111S was cheaper than the standard Series 1 - it had to be a bargain, which as Guy Munday says, 'upset a few people at the time.' The 111S is now quite a desirable version, not that it's readily available today because it was only around for the last year-and-a-half of Series 1 production.

Here's an oddball. The Sport Elise announced in March 1997 and destined for the Autobytel race series had a centrally located driving position and controls. Stylistically, this car was the harbinger of the hard-core Motorsport Elise, announced at the 1999 Earls Court Show and the basis of another one-make series that was part of the BTCC package doing the rounds of UK circuits in 2000; unquestionably it also set the stage for the Exige, launched in April 2000.

Sport Elise had central driving position

The Elise S1. This is a 111S, built between 1999 and 2000

SPECIAL EDITIONS

Besides the standard higher-performance Elise variants, Lotus also released some limited edition models including the Sport 135 (1998/9) with approximately 145bhp and available in different colours and steering wheel, Sport 160 (2000) with 150–160bhp/ 110-117kW and Sport 190 released in 2002. These were more competent on track with their differently rated sports suspension, wheels, tyres and seats according to model. A range of special editions paid testament to Lotus's racing pedigree, such as the 50th Anniversary Edition (green/gold) celebrating 50 years of Lotus cars, the Type 49 ('Gold Leaf' red and white two-tone with gold stripes – reminiscent of the similarly liveried Lotus Elan Sprint), and Type 72 ('JPS' black and gold) that refers to the company's successful F1 Grand Prix car type numbers.

Elise Series 1, Gold Leaf Type 49 livery at Goodwood House, UK

Elise S1, Sport 160 built from 1996 to 2000 was the first real special edition

SPORT 160

The cognoscenti view the Sport 160, brought out towards the end of Series 1 production, as the most desirable car of the entire Series 1 line-up. Originally it was just going to be a 50-units only special produced under the single vehicle rules that applied at the time, although subsequently Lotus got the whole vehicle approved and built more cars. But the first 50 only had to comply with SVA regs and were probably in excess of 160bhp/117kW. Performance had to be stifled a little bit by a change of exhaust to obtain the whole vehicle type approval. As Guy Munday says: 'it was the first real special edition they had done up till then. It had a bit of characteristic popping and banging and burbling built in, a nice set of wheels and an even bigger wing on the back, so it was a car with attitude. But for everybody that liked the way it burbled and banged, there was somebody else who said it was ridiculous, give it 160bhp but make it perfectly smooth, so

a few people missed the point.'

ELISE GT1

I should also mention the Type 115 GT1, an Elise-based sports prototype racing car using a widened Elise chassis and carbon-fibre bodywork. The work's Racing Team rejected the in-house 3.5-litre turbo V8 from the Esprit GT1 in favour of the 6.0-litre Corvette V8 engine. Altogether, eight Elise GT1 race-car chassis were built, with cars run by Fabien Giroix's First Racing for the Lotus factory, with privateers GBF UK and Martin Veyhle Racing running the others. The Elise GT1s were campaigned in the 1997 FIA GT championship alongside proven GT1 offerings from Porsche, Mercedes-Benz, McLaren, Ferrari and TVR. After alternator and gearbox teething troubles the three Lotuses acquitted themselves well enough in the hands of Lammers, Grau and Hezemans, Polican and Prutirat, Badoer and Schiattarella, but though

The Elise Sport 160 engine didn't please everybody

The Elise GT1 at Silverstone, UK

points were scored they failed to build on that modest success. When Proton acquired Lotus Cars in 1998 the GT1 project was dropped. The work's had a third car in hand, intended for use in the British GT championship, which got as far as scrutineering for the Silverstone round in 2000. Toine Hezemans (Mike's father and multiple '70s ETCC champion) drove it on the Supercar Rally 2001 from Paris to Monaco.

ELISE 340R

Another car based on the Series 1 platform is the 340, attractive if you are thinking of venturing down the Caterham or Ariel Atom road, though Guy Munday is not a fan. 'Bearing in mind that technology has moved on, the 340R is still a Rover engine and pushing 190bhp (139kW) through a K-series engine is operating near the edge of the

envelope. We still look after one or two in the workshop, and I think people who own one are genuinely enthusiastic about them. It doesn't do it for me.'

Launched in 2000, just 340 units of the roofless car were produced, and their name and number refer to the 340bhp per tonne power-to-weight ratio of the original 340R prototype which delivered 177bhp while weighing just 500kg (1,100 lb). The final production versions however weighed 568kg (1,250 lb) in race trim. It took the performance through light weight paradigm to its extreme in an optional 190bhp version that everybody went for, in a car with no doors, no windows and no heater. Born of a design study, the 340s futuristic looks were those of a concept car that found its way into production, and it proved a hard sell at £33,000.

The 190hp Lotus 340R at Frédéric Koninckx Motors' Lotus dealership, Antwerp, Belgium

Guy Munday describes it as, 'quite tricky. Reliability of componentry wasn't that great, there were stories about front wings flying off at 90mph, and it's a four hour job to change the battery because you have to take the whole body off.' Expect to pay around £20,000 for a 340R.

EXIGE S1

Inspired by the racing Elises competing in the Autobytel one-make race series of the late 1990s, the Exige (N/A or normally-aspirated)

was launched in April 2000 at Brands Hatch, to coincide with the first practice for the opening Autobytel Race Championship race of the season. It remained in production until the Series 1 Elise was phased out. Bristling with on-track attitude, the Exige's coupe bodywork was like an Elise on steroids, with purposeful beetle-back coupé bodywork, 'rooster comb' style of overhead engine air intake, rear wing and front splitter, though in normal format it shared its soft-top sibling's 1.8-litre Rover K-Series engine, albeit in VHPD (Very High Performance Derivative) tune. It produced 177bhp (132kW; 179PS) in standard form and 192bhp (143kW; 195PS) in the 'track spec' version.

The Exige Series 1 was fairly difficult to sell at the time, coming in the dying days of the Series 1's lifecycle. Customers had to be incentivised by limited editions – for instance a Millennium Edition in 2000. Of the 700 Exiges made in Series 1 format, around 400 stayed in the UK. That makes a Series 1 Exige pretty expensive, starting at £20,000 and going up to £30,000.

The Exige S1 was inspired by the Elises racing in one-make series in the late 1990s

Elise Series 2

Announced on October 9, 2000, the Series 2 Elise was a redesigned Series 1 using a slightly modified version of the Series 1 chassis and the same K-series engine with a brand new Lotus-developed ECU. Initially Series 1 (S1) and Series 2 (S2) cars shared many parts, including the chassis, although they came to have totally different drivetrains when Lotus embraced the Toyota powerplant.

With Russell Carr now heading the styling studio, the new body design paid homage to Lotus's stillborn M250 project and was the first Lotus to be designed on computer. The Series 2 has a much more aggressive demeanour than the classically inspired Series 1 with its cheeky front façade. To achieve the desired effect tiny modifications were made to the chassis. Lotus pruned some side seals away to make entry and exit a little bit easier, while the body styling was sharpened up with much more edgy styling cues, especially in the headlight clusters and knife-edge front wing tops and side air intakes.

Here's the great divide in Elisedom; in single marque terms the Series 2 is a quantum leap from its forebear. For a start it is much better built - warranty statistics prove it; not far into S2 production, the cost of parts and time spent in rectification was halved compared to the Series 1. Constructed in a new factory building on a production line alongside the VX220/Opel Speedster (dropped in 2004), the whole plant was geared to build a General Motors product and so all manufacturing systems had to comply with General Motors' rigorous quality control standards. According to Guy there was a slight price to pay: 'to a small degree it compromised the car's performance as the S2 was slightly heavier, although there was much more scope for tailoring.'

An innovation for Lotus was that the body shells – clamshells in Lotus parlance - themselves were, and still are, supplied by SOTIRA, a French conglomerate who have been producing all Lotus clamshells and certain other panels for the last few years using the RTM (resin transfer moulding) process that is basically a variation of the VARI (vacuum assisted resin injection) system Lotus used to use for the Esprit. The advantages of this method are that woven or random fibreglass mat can be moulded in a low two-minute cycle time, giving constant thickness of material and the facility to produce undercut lips or rims.

When the Series 2 Elise went on sale in 2001 two option packs were available – a first for Lotus; Race Tech, a bare aluminium style statement, and Sports Tourer, more comfortable with leather interior and sound baffling. Guy was surprised by the take up: 'I remember going to a dealer meeting when the car was launched and Lotus explained the differences between the two option packages, and we assumed 80-percent of customers would go for Race Tech and a few softies would choose the less hard-core version. Race Tech came along first but although we had a queue of people waiting to buy the car they all said. "Well, actually we will wait till the Sports Tourer comes out."' It was the complete reverse of what had been expected; about 80-percent were specified as Sports Tourers and about 20-percent were Race Tech. As Guy says, 'with carpets, sound-deadening and a stereo in an Elise, Mazda MX5, Honda S2000 and Boxster people could

The Series 2 Elise was announced in October 2000

be tempted into the Lotus fold.' So although the S2 is visually harder-edged than the S1, it is easier to live with because of cockpit access, materials, fixtures and fittings and creature comfort options.

The Series 2's specification remained untouched until 2004 when Lotus fitted the Toyota 2ZZ-GE 1.8-litre twin-cam engine in the top-of-the-range 111R. That still left The Elise 120 and 160 Rover powered cars in the line-up, and the two engine makes ran concurrently in the range for just over 18 months, from March 2004 to the end of 2005. However, the mooted Toyota-powered 111RS flagship car caused a certain amount of problems for the Rover-powered cars. Guy Munday explains: 'There hadn't been a problem with engine supply or reliability issues, but customer perception of the Rover product fell through the floor to the point where there was a real fight to get customers into Rover-engined cars. But without the K-series powered cars, in '05 and '06 Lotus would have been left with just a single model line-up.' There was a considerable price hike with the first Toyota engined cars, with the standard Elise 120 up around £24,000, a 111S with 160bhp cost about £28,000 and the 190 with a Toyota engine coupled to a six-speed gearbox was on sale at £32,000.

Elise S2 Type 25, Blackrock Sands, Wales, UK

Elise S2, Federal spec, Lotus Peformance Driving School, Spring Mountain, Las Vegas, 2007

ELISE S

The Elise S, still with the K-series power unit, was introduced in April 2005 to replace the 120 and 160 Rover-engined cars, which were phased out at the end of the year. At 140bhp/103kW it filled the gap in the range between the 120 and 160 Rover-engined cars. In 2007 the Elise S became the new base model, but now a Toyota-sourced 1.8-litre engine, the 1ZZ-FE, replaced the K-series Rover engine. The Toyota unit produced 134bhp/98kW at 6200rpm, an increase over the similar capacity 120bhp/88kW Rover engine. However, it was a heavier engine, and along with the addition of airbags, ABS brakes, electric windows, and carpet, weight was increased to 860 kg (1,896 lb), approximately 85 kg (190 lb) more than its predecessor.

For 2008, Lotus continued to make a normally-aspirated Elise S alongside the supercharged SC. Although the car looked much like other Series 2 models, the cockpit now featured a driver and passenger airbag, and ProBax seats gave proper spinal support and better seat-cushion padding. The dashboard was coated Sensasoft, a material that gave a sleek finish without resorting to the leather look. A starter button and new instrument cluster (white on black instead of vice versa), were complemented by intelligent progressive shift warning lights which flashed a sequence of three warnings as the 8500 red line loomed on the tacho.

In 2009, three models were available in Europe: the Elise S with a 134bhp/98kW, 1.8-litre Toyota 1ZZ-FE engine and 5-speed manual gearbox, capable of 0-60 mph in 5.8s and top speed of 127mph (204 km/h); the Elise R with a 189bhp, 1.8-litre Toyota 2ZZ-GE engine and 6-speed manual gearbox, doing 0-60 mph in 4.9s, and top speed of 148mph (238km/h); and the Elise SC, described below. No new models appeared for 2010, though improvements were made to CO_2 emissions and fuel economy.

The 2011 model year Elise range was released at the 80th Geneva Show in 2010,

Federal spec Elise S. Persian Blue is always a popular colour!

European spec Elise 111R, powered by the Toyota 189hp/139kW twin-cam

featuring fresh styling cues incorporating new front clamshell and new cast and forged wheels. There was a twin-spine engine cover and the diffuser was wrapped by a new bumper design incorporating the rear number plate. All-in-one integrated headlights included LED daylight running lights and LED direction indicators, and aerodynamics were improved by a 4-percent reduction in drag coefficient. The rear boot could now be opened from the cockpit rather than by a separate key function. Vehicle warranty was increased to three years or 36,000 miles.

Most significant introduction was the new entry-level 1.6-litre Toyota Valvematic engine, developing 134bhp/98kW at 6,800 rpm and 160Nm/118 lbft torque at 4,400 rpm, returning 46 mls/gall (6.1l/100km or 38 mls/USgall) and CO_2 emissions reduced by 13 per cent. This performance gave the Elise the lowest CO_2 per performance for any petrol-fuelled sportscar in the world. The new engine was mated to a new 6-speed manual gearbox, replacing the old 5-speed box. For the first time, cruise control was available, operated via a stalk on the steering column.

111R / FEDERAL ELISE

To clear up any confusion right away, the 111R is the Euro car and the so-called Federal Elise is the American version. The 2006 Series 2 Elise was powered by the all-aluminium, 189bhp/139kW 1.8-litre Toyota engine with its Yamaha-designed twin-cam head and variable valve timing on intake and exhaust valve gear, driving through a 6-speed manual Toyota gearbox. The best version of the Elise to date, road tests produced acceleration figures of 0–60 mph (0–100 km/h) in 4.9sec or 4.7sec with the Sport Package. The engine management computer is a Lotus programmed unit, and a cam-timing shift at 6,200rpm gives a radical power boost.

Back in 1957, North America was Lotus's first overseas market, and the marque has always retained a dedicated following across the pond. Stymied by complicated vehicle legislation and public liability issues, the 2005 Elise was the first model year to go on sale in the United States, with deliveries starting in the summer of 2004. Type approval required the intervention of the National Highway

Traffic Safety Administration (NHTSA) who provided a three-year exemption for the car as it had yet to meet US bumper and headlight height regulations.

This model was followed by the 2006 Elise 111R and Sport Racer models, and Lotus made a limited edition (50 in the US) version called the Elise Sport. 2006 models also differ from the 2005 models in that they were equipped with LED tail lights, an updated ECU, improved economy and more comfortable ProBax seats.

All Elises manufactured after January 1st 2007 included the new sealed headlamp units and 2.5mph (4.0 km/h) front bumpers required by US federal standards, although they were effectively concealed in the panelwork. For the 2007 model year the LOTUS name on the rear of the vehicle, which previously consisted of flat stickers, was changed to raised lettering.

In order to comply with US federal bumper restrictions, the frontal crash structure was slightly changed and embryonic rear bumpers were added next to the number plate mount,

although around 100 units of the 2007 model year cars were shipped from Hethel to the US without these bumper changes. Also in 2007 the Elise S was released and the 111R renamed the Elise R.

ELISE SC

For 2008, Lotus built a second version of the Elise, the Elise SC, to run alongside a new normally aspirated model, with the same easy riding cockpit. With a non-intercooled Rootes-type Eaton supercharger producing 218bhp/163 kW developed in-house by Lotus Engineering. With no intercooler to weigh it down, the Elise SC lost 8kg/17.6lb compared with its supercharged Exige S stablemate, and as far as horsepower and torque were concerned, the Elise SC gave much the same sort of figures as its coupe cousin. The Elise SC was distinguishable from its normally aspirated sibling by its rear spoiler borrowed from the Type 72 edition, together with new wheels – plus it had the knock-on bonus of decent visibility through the rear windscreen.

The Eaton supercharger cut the Elise SC's

Elise SC Series 2, 2008. The author on the roads above Barcelona

0-60mph to an impressive 4.3 seconds, from the base model's 4.9 seconds, or 4.7 seconds for the Elise plus Sport package, Weight remained a claimed 901kg/1,987lb; just 1.4kg/3lbs more than the previous model. The SC finally ran out of speed at 150mph (240 km/h). I can personally verify this cracking pace, having had the dubious pleasure of maxing out on an unrestricted German autobahn in one. I say dubious, because although safe enough, it isn't what these cars are built for; put them on writhing two-lane blacktop for the most blistering fun. Or better still, the Nürburgring Nordschleife.

2-ELEVEN

Bereft of weather protection and home comforts, this Elise-derived car is a track-day special, though it's road legal so you can drive it to and from the circuit. It took just 11 weeks for Lotus to work up the 2-Eleven from a clean sheet of paper to fully operational machine, and it was launched at the centenary celebrations of Shelsley Walsh hillclimb in 2005. Starting as a basic car with an extensive range of options, it can be tailored for a specific race series anywhere in the world and has been the most successful circuit car ever produced by Lotus in

marketing terms, with around 300 units sold by 2010. I passengered Zandvoort race school instructor Yannick Dillen, fast lady extraordinaire, for a dozen laps in her 2-Eleven. Such is the 2-Eleven's ferocious competence on a winding track that, even wearing full harness, I still clutched the side tube of the roll cage to keep out of her way as she shifted in and out of corners. 'Impressive, isn't it?' she commented afterwards. 'It's light on the steering, and with the semi-slick Yokohamas you can drive on the road, so it's really good fun! I'm using all the ratios, and I do some left-foot braking to influence the nose of the car, force it down to make it steer a bit better, and that works because you have a little bit more weight on the front, and then all of a sudden it turns in.' Out on the track all this seems instantaneous as her feet dance on the pedals, arms twirling from lock to lock, hand darting to-and-fro from steering wheel to gear lever. Poetry in motion. Not so cheap though – a case of less is more. A used 2-Eleven costs from £27,000 to £43,000.

LIMITED EDITIONS

The Series 2 was available as the 111S model with VVC engine technology, though this was discontinued for the 2005 model year when

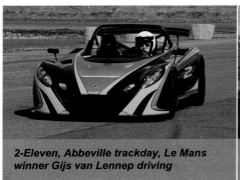

2-Eleven, Abbeville trackday, Le Mans winner Gijs van Lennep driving

Eco Elise S2 was a one-off using green materials including hemp

Exige Cup 260, produced in the 2010 model year, was outstanding on track

the K-series engine was abandoned in favour of the 1.8-litre Toyota powerplant.

Two more track-focussed versions of the Series 2 were available, the 135R and Sport 190, delivering 135bhp/99kW and 192bhp/141kW respectively. These also came with handling upgrades including Lotus Sport Suspension and wider wheels with Yokohama Advan A048 tyres. In certain markets, the 135R was replaced by the Sport 111, which was similar, apart from deploying the 156bhp/114kW VVC engine in place of the 135bhp/99kW K-series.

Like the Series 1's Type 49 Gold Leaf special edition, the Series 2 produced a few limited editions commemorating famous Lotus F1 racing cars. These included the Type 23 (white with two green stripes over the top),

Type 25 (British Racing Green with paired yellow stripes), Type 72 (JPS black and gold livery), Type 99T (Camel yellow), Elise Club Racer (pale blue) and Exige Club Racer (white with green stripes). They were made in batches of between 25 to 100 units each, identified by a little plaque on the dashboard for authentication.

EXIGE SERIES 2

In 2004 the Series 2 Exige was announced, powered by the 1.8-litre Toyota engine, and the following year output rose from 190bhp/139kW to 243bhp/178kW in 2005, with the small run (50 units, in either yellow or black only) supercharged Exige 240R, harbinger of the supercharged Exige S that debuted in February 2006. It deployed the frontal design cues of the Series 2 Elise, revved up with a front splitter, rear wing and air-scooped beetle back coupe shape to give it an added sense of purpose. 'It was always the plan that Exige would always have a small power advantage over Elise,' says Guy, 'which combined with the aerodynamics package, racetrack appearance and feel should give it a premium.' But in fact as the Elise SC moved onto 240bhp/176kW it could match the Exige's performance. Values are more straightforward than for the S1 Exige, apart from one-offs, like the Red Bull GT3 Exige, built and raced by Lanzante Motorsport (with input by Adrian Newey) in Britcar and other endurance series. Priced at £130,000, that 345bhp/253kW beast could even be used on the road. More relevantly, prices for Series 2 Exiges sought by us

Exige S was 'absolutely bullet proof and fairly vice free'. The Type 72 (here) also had a legendary look

mere mortals start at £17,000 and rise to £45,000 for the newest Exige S.

EXIGE S
Recalling the heavily gunned, lightly-armoured German pocket battleships of World War 2, the Exige S is the pocket supercar. It was first produced in 2006 and is described by Guy Munday as, 'absolutely bullet proof, fairly vice free. It is not an overly stressed engine.' He says, 'and the supercharger is not over-powerful, given that Lotus have raced with in excess of 300bhp (220kW).' On the 2009 trans-Holland Dutch Spring Run I found the Exige 260 S very thirsty, without trying hard, and of course even more with the turbo on full boost on the autobahn. It proved a good, comfortable companion going down to Abbeville for some trackday action though, even on the autoroute.

THE EXIGE 270E TRI-FUEL
Here's a curved ball. The Exige 270E Tri-

Lotus Exige 270E Tri-fuel could run on gasoline, ethanol or methanol

fuel launched at the 2008 Geneva Show was hailed as a quantum leap in alternative fuelling, with its unique capability to run on gasoline, ethanol or methanol. But in this case pleasure wasn't sacrificed to virtue. The 270Es performance is blink-and-you-miss-it fantastic; it takes a mere 3.8sec to reach 60mph, warping on to a shade under 160mph before howling 'enough!' So what we have here is the fastest Exige in the range and the fastest road-legal bio-ethanol car ever built. The 270E designation reveals power output, up 50bhp/37kW over the standard car, and the fact it runs on E for ethanol. That's a hybrid alcohol fuel with motor racing applications. It is made from crop fermentation mixed with gasoline, resulting in a 70 per cent reduction in carbon dioxide emissions.

Lotus Engineering took just five weeks in summer 2006 to re-engineer the supercharged Toyota engine to run on ethanol. The aluminium block Toyota four is standard, but the supercharger and intercooler have been adjusted to cope with the power hike, while the ECU is remapped to handle the new fuel. The inlet manifold's quartet of injectors is bigger, and an additional pair of injectors is installed at the supercharger inlet to augment the fuel entering the engine at higher speeds.

The major obstacle to running any bio-fuel car is accessing the vital fluids – just a handful of UK supermarkets stock bio-fuel at the moment. This could be the way of the future though.

EUROPA S AND SE

Introduced at Geneva in 2005 and in the showrooms for 2006, the Europa S was conceived as a sportscar for Proton but was reabsorbed as an in-house project. Taking its name from the Renault- and Lotus-Ford twin-cam-powered mid-engined Lotus model of the late 1960s, the new generation base model Europa was powered by the 197bhp/145kW 2.0-litre GM turbocharged four. It could do 0-60 mph in 5.6 seconds (0-100 km/h in 5.8 sec.) with a maximum speed of 143mph (230 km/h). The justification for fitting the GM turbo 2.0-litre unit was because the Europa was intended for everyday use, and the unblown Toyota engine was thought to be a little bit frenetic; there's a big step-up in power at 6,000rpm where it all comes alive on the second cam, but you've got to be prepared to drive it quite hard. The Europa on the other hand isn't really designed as a hard car and the turbocharged engine gives more useable power lower down. Two years later the Europa SE version was announced, its power uprated to 222bhp/163kW and cabin more refined. When it first came out, and until the Exige S was introduced at 218bhp/160kW, the upgraded Europa was the most powerful car in the range.

Combining the power of the Elise with something approaching the cabin comfort of the Evora, albeit in two-seater format, the Europa is the least raunchy of the Elise range. The Europa was announced at the same time as Audi relaunched its 4x4 3.2-litre V6 TT, yet it cost £1,000 more than the Audi, giving the press a useful stick with which to berate it. As Guy points out, 'had it been touted as a practical Elise with nicer trim and a big hatchback Lotus might have

got away with it, but they tried to make it a "business class" type of thing, so we were always a little bit on a back foot with that car.' Though private sales are down at £17K, expect to spend between £20K and £30K for a top-line Europa SE. Also based on the same chassis, the Vauxhall/Opel VX220 Speedster employs the same normally-aspirated and turbo drivelines, and while it's far less aesthetically refined than the Europa it is much the same car – in convertible format, with prices from £7,500 to £17,000. So if looks and lacking the Lotus badge don't bother you, it might be worth a thought.

SPECIAL MODELS
Sport 190
Sport 135R
Type 23
Type 25
Type 49
Type 72
Type 99T
Sports Racer
Club Racer
Tri-fuel 270E
California Edition

Cars sharing the Elise platform
- Lotus Europa S
- Lotus 2-Eleven
- Lotus Exige
- Lotus Elise GT1
- Lotus GT3
- Lotus 340R
- Rinspeed sQuba
- Tesla Roadster
- Vauxhall VX220
- Pininfarina Enjoy
- Dodge Circuit

Europa SE, seen here in Marrakech 2009, used a 197hp/145kW 2-litre turbo engine

Performance, looks, heritage – what's not to like about the Elise if you are in the market for a snappy little sports car? Well maybe in the back of your mind there's that old pub-bore adage: LOTUS, Lots Of Trouble, Usually Serious. Fair comment for a 1970 Elan S4, say, but since the introduction of GM quality control processes in 1998, that anxiety can be put to rest. I spoke to a typical owner, Michael Hipperson who runs the Elise Garden Party charity events (in aid of Little Havens Childrens' Hospice) and he's run Elises for ten years with no problems at all. So with that one out of the way, just how to you choose the car for you? First step is to just get in an Elise and drive it. That's what it is gagging for you to do.

Back in 1998 I wrote a book on the design, genesis and construction of the Elise and after I'd been shown the ropes on the Hethel test track by test drivers Dave Minter and Alastair McQueen, press officers Alastair Florance and Prunelier Stuart lent me a couple of cars for a month or so while I scribbled. I thought it was the most exhilarating car I'd ever driven, bar none, even having sampled Caterhams, not to mention Morgans, TVRs and a raft of Porsches ancient and modern. And thanks to supercharged evolutions, that holds true more than a decade later. As a regular contributor to the in-house Lotus Club International magazine I've powered up Elises and Exiges all over Europe and the USA in the course of researching features, drive stories and photoshoots. We've been in the frozen arctic north and the boiling desert south, we've campaigned them on race tracks and the open road, we've steered them through middle-of-nowhere hamlets and the busiest city in the world, and I've pretty much loved them everywhere – as have any roadside bystanders.

There's a Lotus saying that the car should be a 'glove on the hand,' a second skin, and that really means something in an Elise. The car is so responsive, and as a driver you are involved in such a close man/machine physical and mental relationship that you'll pirouette full circle around a roundabout just for the hell of it – and then do it all over again. You'll seek out twisting mountain passes and hill roads just for the thrill of pumping the Elise through hairpin heaven - and then you'll go back for more. Drive alive? I'd say so.

Elise Series 1

The Series 1 is a close contact drive, fingertip sensitive on the steering wheel so that only the smallest input is needed for a change of direction, and any apex can be clipped with spot-on precision. You address the steering wheel with elbows bent and hands at ten-to-two, and for this six-footer, that means a reasonably straight-legged seating position pushing you back into the seat, with the right knee nestling comfortably against the side of the chassis. The driver's seat is biased towards the centreline of the car, and the passenger seat is immovably fixed further back. You feel it in your fingers, you feel it in your toes - throttle response is instantaneous, and the car rips away from traffic lights in second and third gear. The 1.8-litre K-series performance is athletic at low speed, scintillating on bendy country roads, and more than adequate on fast A- roads. It's a gutsy engine, and quite adequate for the car in standard trim, although a rasping exhaust note might have made the heart race that little bit faster. The Elise can idle along at just under 1,000rpm, and at low revs it feels like, well, any small car. Except of course you'll always feel

Elise S2 111S at speed. With 156hp/116kW, it was available from 2002

special, even in traffic, because you're in this little gem of a sports car. But as you increase speed it really beefs up, all the way to 100mph (160km/h).

The S1 Elise isn't designed for motorways, though I have spent long distances on US Interstate and European autoroutes in more modern variants and it's been easily bearable. The ride is taut yet far from uncomfortable, but the rear end does respond with a bonk if you take on a pothole or similar abrupt depression. The suspension is pretty noisy on undulating rural back roads, but there's no hint of the scuttle shake that still bedevils some wannabe sports cars and cabriolets. The brakes are fiercely efficient and confidence inspiring. You know they are going to anchor up safely approaching any imminent challenges, and that encourages you to negotiate them with proper vigour.

Elise S1, Rachel Larratt and Steve Warwick on La Carrera Panamericana

EASE OF ACCESS

The Spartan cockpit focuses your concentration on the matter at hand. There's a purity about the bare, uncarpeted aluminium chassis defining the body of the interior, but its intimacy is reassuringly womb-like. Getting in and out requires traditional sports car contortionism. Support your body weight by clutching the side of the chair and the sill (rocker), then get your backside and inside leg in first before swinging your other leg in. To manoeuvre yourself out, push yourself up using the side of the passenger seat to obtain leverage; extract your outer leg, holding onto the steering wheel with your inner hand while the other hand supports your weight on the sill; when your outer foot is on the ground, bring your other leg over so you're sitting on the

sill, and lift yourself out. Not really the pantomime it might suggest, but hardly a quick get away.

Once in the driving seat though, the controls are well laid out and accessible, with about 3in (75mm) between the steering wheel and the gear lever – the width of outstretched thumb to little finger. The light-control stalk (this is the Series 1, remember) and two-speed wiper switches are right where you need them and the window winder is just 6in (150mm) from the wheel. The light buttons are activated by a single push.

There's an integrated electronic speedo and tachometer system by Stack instruments with multifunction LCD display, and the dials are appropriately minimalist. The speedo is on the right, calibrated in mph and km/h, and the rev-counter on the left. There are warning lights under the speedometer, and fuel and temperature symbols are below the rev-counter. The digital petrol gauge reads 75 litres (16.5 imp.galls/19.8 US galls) when the tank is full.

Air con? Hmmm. I believe it does sap engine power slightly, though the compressor is relatively small so as not to compromise the car's light weight. So it's a mixed blessing and even then not that efficient in hot climate running. The odometer and trip are in a little space to the left and all are housed in the single binnacle clearly visible through the top half of the steering wheel. The radio antenna is mounted behind the rear window, and in case you have an In-Car Entertainment system fitted by your dealer, Lotus supply a couple of trim sections to go either side of it on the dash panel.

To hold the S1 engine cover up you simply prop it open with the luggage compartment cover. Luggage space is better than you might expect, and there's room for a holdall or smallish suitcase, but this is compromised if you need to accommodate the soft top. The cant rails and cross bars stow away neatly enough behind the seats, and if you're pushed for space the hood could probably be tucked away there too. There's also a net behind the seats to enclose other small personal effects so they don't fly around when you're on the move.

Elise Series 2

On the road, modern Elise S2s feel pretty much like the S1 - the same but newer. Certain aspects of the controls have evolved or become more sophisticated, like the light switches, now push buttons to the right of the steering column, plus starter button. I drove a 2007 Elise out of Barcelona and on into the Montserrat Mountains, and on a section of fast, shallow bends where the cambers were all over the place the car tracked superbly, sticking tight to the road with no kickback from the steering wheel. Through a 20km section of hairpins it was such fun that my face wore a permanent grin. I found I could be relaxed with it as well,

establishing a rhythm and flowing through the turns, even though each one was subtly different. Later, doing 80mph on an undulating motorway, the S2's primary ride proved excellent - the front and rear suspension can go up and down at the same time. It's testimony to the ability of the car's suspension to come up in rebound and settle in rebound so there is no overshoot back down again. A poor primary ride means it would be bucking and you'd start to feel car sick if the frequency was wrong. Secondary ride is the ability to go over broken surfaces effectively, and on these the Elise behaved itself well.

ELISE 1.6

Launched in April 2010, the newest Elise incorporates subtly revised styling cues: the teardrop headlamp nacelles house LED lights and indicators so the front panel contours are cleaner, while twin driving lamps live either side of the radiator grille, flanked by a pair of moustache shaped intakes that boost the family resemblance with the Evora. A similar stylistic spruce-up has taken place round the back too, the one-piece rear panel and diffuser giving the impression of a broader car than before. Like the front 'bonnet' panel, the engine-cover ribbing is also revised. The official stats show that the new

Elise S2, Federal spec. The author giving it some in Florida

Elise S2 at an Abbeville (France) on the edge at a trackday, May 09

Elise's green credentials are well in order and, in fact, it's the cleanest sportscar on the market, with the lowest CO2 emissions in its category. Price-wise, it came in at a very reasonable £27,450 in the UK. Most significantly, it's powered by the 134bhp, 1,598cc Toyota twin-cam unit and matching six-speed gearbox. It was interesting to find that on a drive in the south of France though 200cc smaller than its Elise R stablemate, the 876kg entry-level car could be just as much – perhaps more – of a hoot than its 1.8 siblings.

En route to Monaco for the 2010 Historic Grand Prix I drove the new 1.6 Elise on some of the finest driving roads in Europe, specifically La Route Napoleon and the Gorge du Verdon in the Alpes Maritimes of southeast France. It's no coincidence that the Monte Carlo Rally uses stretches of it between special stages, and photographer Antony Fraser and I took a leaf out of their tulips route book to air the Elise. We headed southeast from Valence to where the Route Napoleon hooks up into the Alps at Digne-les-Bains on the N85, and from here on in, the nimble Lotus came into its own.

It's only 19km (13 miles) from the Castellane turn-off to the start of the spectacular Gorge du Verdon, a sprawling landmass of gigantic conical hills, exposed strata thrusting dramatically skywards containing the swirling Verdon river till it spews from its chasm into the Lac de Sainte Croix. Rockfalls are a perpetual hazard, creating mini chicanes along the way and requiring constant monitoring by a truck-mounted blade that shoves the debris aside. The road tracks the Verdon River a hundred feet below, sliced into the cliff as if by a cheese wire. We've got the top off and as we pass beneath dramatic rock overhangs I straight-line the Elise through the bends. We emerge from a defile in the cliffs and there's the exhilarating sight of the unfeasibly blue lake, stretching out way down below. The

road zigzags its way down to the lakeside and, despite frequent rock falls, the blacktop is remarkably good, allowing fluent progress through the incessant bends. This is Lotus driving at its purest. There's no power steering on the Elise, yet you have fingertip control of the wheel for fine adjustments. Turn-in is as exact as can be, rounding every kind of corner you could wish for, aiming at apexes, just shy of kissing the stone walls, and there's much arm twirling, feeding the wheel from lock to lock in the hairpins – and here a firm grip on the rim is necessary. The taut chassis and finely wrought wishbone suspension and dampers, complemented by gripping Yokohama tyres, give absolute handling precision. Hugging the rock face, I floor the accelerator, snatch 3rd and blast down to the next turn, braking in a straight line and double-declutch for 2nd and steer into the curve, me and the Lotus united.

The new Elise's 0-60mph time is 6.0-seconds, and it's no slouch on the Autoroute either, a 90mph cruiser if you want, returning 34mpg and 400 miles to a tankful of 95-octane. But at high revs it's a real performance car. The 1.6 Toyota unit has a noticeable change in pace at 4,800rpm when a flap shortens the inlet tract length, giving a slight dip in engine tone. Be warned, chasing this subtle song shift can be addictive, and I find myself jumping at opportunities to push through the magic 4,800rpm barrier in the knowledge that more bhp and torque are instantly on tap. In fact it loves to rev all the way till 7,000 when the limiter kicks in and red lights flash on the tachometer. Snarl morphs to roar as the revs rise, a four-pot banshee blare at max-out, an aural attack. Bring on the cliffs for utmost echo.

We've come a fair way now, and the car's Pro-Bax seats are still providing decent support so there's no excuse for slumping. Top off, the one-ness with the elements is complete. And

Left: Elise 1.6 – testing the cabin for leaks in Provence! Right: Trying hard in an Elise SC S2 near Catalonia

that's never truer than when it rains, which it does now. Having stashed the top behind the seats in deference to camera bags in the boot, we manage to unfurl it over our heads and click the side-rails into place to make it taut without so much as getting out of the car. The air-con makes short work of the steamed-up windscreen in the re-canopied cockpit.

After Grasse we take the final plunge down to Vence, and we're done. Umbrella pines, spiky aloes and banana palms spell Côte d'Azur, the Med's a dozen clicks away and it's a short hop to the cosy comforts of the Mas de Pierre hotel.

The 1.6 version complements the Elise range absolutely. It deserves more than entry level status because it's Lotus motoring at its purest: a high revving engine that needs to be worked hard for best effect, yet it's willing as anything when you ask it to perform. Its spellbinding agility is a given. You have to work the gears more, rev the engine harder than the 1.8 versions, and that makes it a more involving car – hard concentration makes for swiftest progress and it's reminiscent of the '60s Elan. The controls are laid out perfectly to achieve this, though your right foot needs to behave as

smoothly as possible while it slides from accelerator to brake and back again. It's a really nifty car, the 1.6 Elise.

ELISE SC

The supercharged Elise SC of 2008 is significantly quicker than earlier and normally aspirated versions (as is its similarly equipped stablemate the Exige S). You immediately register the torque, and it gels completely with the flexibility that's always been a feature of the model's performance, even at a lowly 2000rpm in 5th when negotiating narrow village streets. It pulls straightaway without the need to find 6000rpm for the second cam to come into play. It's such an able car, power is accessible on demand. You can be tooling along in 4th or 5th and if you want to have a little squirt to get out of somebody's way or to overtake, it's right there; you haven't got to screw it up to 4000rpm to get a result. As a result, turns you might take in 2nd in a normally aspirated car, you can now do easily in 3rd; nothing to do with gearing, there's just more torque available. And you've got both hands on the wheel instead of chopping gears.

But if you're progressing from an Elise to the

supercharged SC, you need some driver re-education. It's a good lesson, trying to be in a gear higher than you would expect to be in an S or an R. In either of those you want to keep the revs up to stay in their high power band, but that's not how it works in the SC. However, this ability to perform at lower revs doesn't make the SC more economical than an S or an R, since in your drive cycle you'll do plenty of different sorts of driving and with more power and torque you'll naturally use more fuel. Comparing the relative power bands, taking the SC to about 6,200rpm, which is where the second cam comes in on the R, the SC is really flying in 5th and it's the supercharger that's done the hard work. There's a nice linear progression without having to work the gears, which you'd need to do in an R.

Exige

Harder edged than the Elise, the Exige's controls have a refreshing immediacy: a flick of the wrist to change direction, tiny steering inputs weave the car through the bends, with similarly flexible wrist action shifting the lever between 3rd, 4th and 5th. Nimble footwork brings instant advance and retard. The Exige's flat handling and sharp turn-in are pure pleasure. On a winding A-road the Lotus delivers ferocious performance, and in 4th and 5th you feel you can move mountains; it's incredibly quick and peerless in its responsiveness to steering, accelerating and braking.

The supercharged version, the Exige S, is the stealth bomber of the range. You'd never accuse the standard Exige or Elise of impotence, but the S's supercharger endows it with fresh virility, transforming the delicacy of the original car's power delivery into something even more potent. It is all about the sophistication of the supercharger's power delivery; sharp yet seamless.

The Exige S truly comes alive on the curvaceous EU funded motorways that populate southern Europe, straight-lining the bends on largely traffic free toll roads. And the blown S can be set up with launch control dialled in to the throttle – press the 'on' button, set the required rpm, engage clutch, press the accelerator to rev limiter, drop the clutch and the Exige S is propelled off the line at maximum velocity. That aluminium thimble on the left of the steering column? Say you're on a skid pan, and you want to increase or decrease the oversteer, you keep your wheel in the same position and twist the thimble a notch or two till you find the amount of opposite lock you're comfortable with. Now that's real driving. Acceleration is exceedingly rapid, the car leaping gazelle-like from a standstill and rushing eagerly forward into whatever series of turns you have in store for it. The soundtrack is equally awesome, the supercharger providing a whistling accompaniment to the exhaust's angry rasp, with the transmission whine on backing vocals as we blast through the tunnels. At 4,000rpm in 5th gear it starts to really pull, hurling you forward at warp speed, but try it on the everyday highway, cluttered with restrictions, and it's just as pleasurable. The car's handling ability means you can go around any corner at 35mph without lifting, revelling in the instant throttle response, the sharpness of the brakes, the turn-in, the knotchiness of the gearshift.

From the driving seat of the Exige S, the reality of that fresh dose of power is that the supercharger's air intake and plumbing takes up all the room under the beetle-back so there's absolutely no visibility in the mirror above the windscreen. You rely totally on the door mirrors either side. This makes reversing quite an art – it's essential to know exactly where the back of the car is – but that's probably a price worth paying.

Exige S comes alive on the curvaceous EU motorways of southern Europe

The Lotus Europa SE, seen here in Morocco's Atlas Mountains

Europa

I drove an SE version from Stuttgart to Marrakech and the Atlas Mountains, then back as far as Barcelona in Spring 2009 – a 3,000 mile trip - and I really resented giving it back, despite the minor tribulations of bribery, corruption and speed cops en route. The 2.0 turbo GM engine (from the VX/220 Roadster) makes the Europa nearly as quick overall as the Elise SC. There's a deeper, less urgent engine note to the Europa than the blown 1.8 Toyota unit in the Elise, but the turbo kicks in with no lag whatsoever. Acceleration is blistering, and it's not a lot slower than the Elise SC from 0-to-60mph in 5.5s and whistling up to 145mph, working slickly through its close ratio six-speed 'box. Short-shifting out of the tollbooths on the French autoroutes there was that funny little whistle every time I lifted off the accelerator, like water gurgling down the sink. As a measure of limit-abiding fuel economy, an Autoroute tank-full got me from Orange in Provence to Barcelona, 430kms (267 miles) in four hours – averaging 106kph (66mph). On an exhilarating climb over a small mountain pass towards Grenada, winding tightly to the summit, the Europa steamed up it peerlessly. These were wonderful roads for a Lotus, switching this way and that, through long, fast curves. I glimpsed 180kph

tracking through the turns, it was so very taut and poised, hyper-responsive to steering inputs, but you can also control the turn-in by lift-off oversteer: off the throttle, it tucks in, back on the throttle the nose comes out again.

Styled as a Grand Tourer and designed in-house at Hethel by Barney Hatt, the Europa's frontal aspect has more in common with Evora than Elise. The roofline is higher than its siblings – just as the sills are cutaway for ease of access, and the rear clams have less rounded, more angled wheel arches than the junior Hethel line-up. It has a comfortable leather accented upholstered cabin, and there's neat stitching on the dashboard and atop the main instruments. The seats are adequately padded and covered in leather to harmonise with the door liners. The main instruments are set in their own twin binnacle, cowled like medieval monks, as are the fascia air vents. The levers and switchgear is GM, as seen in Elise and Exige, plain but functional. As well as the parcel tray there are several useful pockets for oddments, even in the roof headlining, plus those minimal sun visors, four huge speakers, an infuriatingly hard-to-access cup-holder between the seats, and a cigarette lighter socket where I plugged in my sat-nav.

Buying an Elise Series 1

Unless it happens to be a low mileage car, let's say below 40,000 miles, you'll probably be flying solo buying a Series 1, viewing privately owned cars and specialists' forecourts. Guy Munday describes the market: 'if you are looking for a typical Series 1 now, they are around £7-8-9,000, typically with about 40-50-60,000 miles, at least three or four owners and they've probably fallen out of main dealer servicing.' Guy recently had in part exchange a one owner from new car with just 9,000 miles and a service history, but that's the exception that proves the rule, since he barely sells any Series 1 Elises these days. That's not to say you are bound to go privately: just look on Pistonheads and there are several specialists advertising regularly: JSD Racetech, Bell & Colvill, Pure Lotus, Frosts, Castle Lotus, Alexander David, Adrian Blyth, Will Blackham, Hi-torq, Williams, and so on. I've listed other dedicated specialists in the appendix.

EARLY PRODUCTION CARS

In particular, Guy keeps well away from first production year cars built in 1996, because as he says, 'it was all brand new technologies and hand-built, and they used to rattle and squeak. Into 1997, they still banged and creaked but after that they were all fairly consistent.'

In 2010 it was possible to find an Elise Series 1 online for as little as £5,000, rising to £15,000 tops. But you may be better off buying a car from specialists (in the UK, from dealers like Paul Matty or Kelvedon Motors), who, though less likely to offer cheap Series 1s, do have access to decent cars that are outside the main Lotus dealer network.

HIGH PERFORMANCE SERIES 1S

The Sport 135 and 111S are both more desirable than the standard Elise, because of improved specification and comparative rarity. But topping Guy's list would be the Sport 160, and more specifically, one of the first 50 cars

The author enjoying the Elise on the open roads of Spain

produced; 'if you can get one of the first 50, and that is verifiable via the chassis number, then that is quite a rare car and a nice thing to have these days. In good condition they are worth having, that's for sure.'

The premium between a standard car and a 111S is probably £500, while the 160 already has a cult following, so expect to shell out close to £12,000 for one of the those rarified first 50 units. Greg Lock of UK specialist tuners Hangar 111 agrees with Guy regarding the Sport 160. For him, desirable models within the Elise range are the Sport 160, the special edition Types 49 and 72 and all the derivatives – the 135, 160, 111S. 'The 111S is obviously a lot more powerful; it's 150bhp compared to the standard car's 120bhp. It's got a big valve engine, the VVC unit that is controlling the inlet cam. But the one for me would be the Sport 160, it's a bit more quirky, the engine is a bit more hunty on tickover. Its a pretty car, a different take on the theme.'

THE SERIES 1 EXIGE

Since its April 2000 debut at Brands Hatch, England, enthusiasm has grown for the Series 1 Exige. Only 400 of these models were sold in the UK. As Guy Munday points out, 'it is quite a cult car these days, and if you can find one that has not been got at or raced it's worth considering – values are holding up well. The pool of cars that you can draw from is diminishing all the time because they are all being used, abused and written off as time goes by and they're not building any more.' There are rumours that build quality wasn't all it might have been. 'It was probably hurried through and so it rattled and creaked a little bit, maybe.' Just like a real racing car, then. But don't forget to insist on air conditioning, vital for a car where you can't

An early Elise S1 requires careful selection

A faster S1 would be the 111S (1999-2002)

Series 1 Exige has become quite a cult car

Elise S2 – here in Indianapolis at LOG 29 2008 – build quality is consistently good

take the roof off. 'Give it 10, 15 or 20 years and I think the Series 1 Exige will be an icon,' says Guy. Could be an investment as a collector's car.

The Series 2 Elise

In terms of quality control you don't have to look quite as hard at Series 2s as the Series 1, though there were teething troubles on a few early cars. According to Guy, 'a 1999 car is probably an ex-Lotus development car, which could throw up some anomalies; year 2000 ones did rattle a bit when they went over bumps, but on the whole they are OK. There is also a slightly later generation of Rover engine with Lotus's own mapping on it which made for much smoother running.' The Rover-powered Series 2 Sports Tourers were by far the most popular version when the car was new, and that is still the case today.

On the forecourt the Race Tech version is less desirable, but you can always dress it up with a set of floormats and a radio if it ticks all the other buyer boxes. The Toyota engine marked a watershed in the reliability stakes. 'To this day we have never had a Toyota engine failure,' reflects Guy. 'They are rock solid.' If you do go for a Rover-powered car, remember the caveats listed under buying advice for the Series 1.

Guy is confident about Series 2 build quality: 'Sometimes cars betray their hand-built, built-on-a-budget background, but the Series 2 is consistently good and that is true of the Exige and 2-Eleven now.' The sophisticated SOTIRA-made S2 clamshells are as good on the underside as the upper side, though repairs are more difficult to effect than panels made by the traditional hand-laid process.

RECENT MODELS

The Elise S, the Series 2 Exige, the supercharged Exige 240R and the Exige S

2 Elevens: Gavin Kirby leads Mark Fullalove In Lotus Elise Trophy

are all relatively young, values are high and they're not plentiful in the marketplace. Depreciation (at least in the UK) is not excessive and brings on the dilemma of deciding whether to buy recent used or pay

not too much more for a new car – which at least will be to your own specification. All the Series 2 limited editions, such as the various Type cars and the Elise and Exige Club racers are desirable, with rarity value and distinctive livery making them a little more expensive than standard cars.

THE EUROPA

Though the Europa proved a hard sell at launch, the effects of depreciation have allowed the car to find a level where it has a following, though selling the new cars can still be difficult. Values are looking good for nearly new cars though, and you get the practicality of easy entry and exit; full leather, sat-nav and air-con as standard; plus a bigger rear storage area. In Guy's opinion, and I agree, it is a great car whose moment has arrived.

Standard full leather, sat-nav and air-con make the Lotus Europa SE attractive

Where to look

There are several very popular seller sites online and these should be be your starting point in the search for an Elise or Exige. In the UK for instance, try Pistonheads (www. pistonheads.co.uk) or Auto Trader (www. autotrader.co.uk). In the USA, sites such as www. cars.com and www.automotive.com list Lotus cars near to you and local resources can often offer more. Cars can range from private end-of-the-road models right up to brand new models.

Ebay, the auction site, is more a way to monitor prices actually achieved than being an appropriate place to purchase a jewel like an Elise. Sellers can now put a car on for a 30-day advert, so it's more of a mainstream sales option, but it can be a frenzied final few minutes as the deal goes down.

Vendors can be enthusiast-led dealerships, both mainline and specialist, plus petrolheads who love their cars – but because of that they usually over-value them. At the risk of teaching grandmothers to suck eggs, you can refine the search for your car by price (low to high and vice versa), by distance from your home post or zipcode and by the age of the advert. That's a good one – a car that's been on the website for several weeks may well be problematic. The big online classified sites are an immediate intro to what's around and how much it costs, but bear in mind that some ads are speculative and may be open to much lower offers.

Always check the car out first, accompanied by a reliable Elise techie. Never buy sight unseen, without first feeling the clams and gassing it up.

Next stop might be Lotus's own used car locator site, Lotus Central, to which any main dealer can contribute stock. And after that check out the independent classified sites.

When it comes to advertising strategy and knowing where to look, it's worth noting that Guy Munday of Strattons is typical of many in that he doesn't advertise in magazines any more. If Lotus have a major feature in one of the top car magazines, you may see some official Lotus sanctioned adverts alongside. Occasionally you may see something in your local press, but it can be worthwhile to arm yourself with a sheaf of the current month's specialist motoring magazines. This could be anything from Octane, Autocar, Road & Track, Car & Driver, etc. and any independent national Lotus clubs (like Club Lotus in the UK) and the factory produced Lotus Club International magazine.

Though hard copy may have faded into the dark ages, Stratton Motor Company make the most of their showroom window facing a busy main road, regularly rotating stock. As Guy says, 'we have traffic lights outside that turn red every 40 seconds and people stop and look in the window. Some people say they've been driving past for years and now the time is right to come in and buy a car. So don't forget to check local specialists.'

WHAT A MAIN DEALER OFFERS

A main dealer car will cost more than a private sale, but as always, you get what you pay for. In most countries, there is legislation to protect private individuals who buy cars from dealers (in the UK used and new car dealers are governed by the Sale of Goods Act, which means they have to supply cars of a reasonable quality with a warranty).

It's worth pointing out that the selling price (compared to trade purchase price on a used car) of a main dealer car is related to the dealer's additional costs, with the benefit of additional security for the buyer. In the UK for instance, they have to pay VAT on the gross margin, that is the difference between the purchase price and the sale price. This is irrespective of whatever costs have been incurred to get the car on sale, which might include servicing, paintwork, or other repairs and later, the cost of advertising and sale. The

comfort factor when stumping up a large purchase price is enhanced by the knowledge that there's a guarantee backed by reputable workshop skills. Guy Munday's expert eye rejects 70 per cent of the cars he is offered, so you need to have a level of engineering proficiency, or at least a very expert friend, to be absolutely confident of saving money by buying privately.

HOW MAIN DEALERS SOURCE NEARLY-NEW CARS

Guy doesn't source his stock from the general motor trade: 'all the cars that I sell are known to me, either because I sold them originally or because we've serviced them. If someone has had two or three services done here it gives you an accurate picture of where the car has been and what it has been up to.'

At one end of the scale the dealer can take a car in and apply a new coat of paint, repair dents, scratches, scrapes and make it look pretty, 'because some young tear-away has had it. But if a cleric has owned it you can be fairly sure it hasn't had a terribly hard life. You get a good feel for the car by talking to the owner.' It's like when you buy a pet dog, he continues, 'you always want to see it with its mother: make sure you see the Elise with its owner.'

Exige Sprint. The high-end cars are available at the better dealerships

Another route into a nearly new car is to go for an ex-demonstrator, or an ex-press fleet or manager's car from the Lotus factory. While a privately owned car with 9,000 miles (15,000km) should be a no brainer, a management-run company car that's done 15,000 miles (24,000km) will at least have been comprehensively serviced, and it will be considerably cheaper than the 1-owner, weekend only car. But Guy is wary, preferring the privately owned cars. 'There is a bit of kudos attached to having Lotus Cars as the only previous owner, because Lotus have their own servicing department and a factory service record is seen to be a nice thing. We are offered the opportunity to buy from a list of ex-management cars by the factory every six weeks, but I rarely take them because generally to get them to a saleable standard usually requires refurbishing wheels, paint and tyres.'

LOTUS SPECIALISTS

The main dealer network mainly sells current cars, but there are Lotus specialists who deal with older, cheaper cars, which fall outside the Lotus approved warranty scheme. The main dealers may often pass cars that don't meet their requirements (or that wouldn't be cost effective to repair) on to certain specialists. Many of these specialists have good relationships with the main dealer network and some are listed in the appendices.

PLAYING THE MARKET – WHEN AND WHERE TO BUY AND SELL

Timing can really work in your favour if you get it right. Play the seasons' game. In the northern hemisphere October and November are traditionally bad months for sellers of convertible sports cars, therefore good months for buyers wanting a good deal. Conversely, March or April are great months for selling a car, and you'll pay

top price if you're buying. The principal is simple: buy when prices and availability are good and sell when availability is down and prices are firmer. That way you mitigate a little bit of depreciation going forwards. As for June and July – forget it. There'll be a reduced selection in the showrooms and the prices will, more likely, still be at their Spring peaks.

It's also worth thinking about location. In some temperate climates, air conditioning won't be a regular feature. As Graeme Robertson of Murray Motors in Scotland (in the UK's north) jokes, 'they don't spec their cars up in Scotland, they keep them as austere as possible because the Scots don't like spending money! Any extra outlay goes into enhanced performance.' His dealership is a stone's throw from Edinburgh airport, and there are several fine cars in his showroom including a rare 340R and a gorgeous Elise in the blue and white Scottish racing colours of Écurie Ecosse. That should sell easily locally. But if you're in London – you might be able to offload a whacky coloured car more easily in part-ex than you would in rural Norfolk.

GETTING YOUR CHOSEN CAR CHECKED OVER

There is absolutely no point in having a mainstream national automobile organization do a pre-purchase inspection on a Lotus Elise. Just watch one of their people try and look up front for the engine and you know you've thrown your money away.

Any decent dealer should make a space and a ramp available for a specialist who knows the brand to look at the car, especially if they think they are going to get the subsequent servicing work.

THE FOUR RULES

Guy Munday has four principle rules for buying a Lotus, and they are worth applying yourself

Beware of wacky colour schemes!

when you begin your hunt.

1. *Colour and specification;* does it meet your requirements? Not too radical? Can you easily re-sell?

2. *Number of owners;* too many? Is there something wrong with the car? Too little usage? So does it need recommissioning?

3. *Evidence of crash damage;* it's all about how it's been used – and repaired!

4. *Servicing;* does the car have a decent level of service documentation, and who has been looking after it?

COLOUR AND SPECIFICATION

Colour is one of the fundamentals of value and saleability. By definition, the more obscure the colour, the fewer people there are who will want to own it – though the ones that do may be super keen! Guy currently has a pink Elise in his showroom, 'which I didn't order,' he hastens to add. It will be more tricky to sell because not many people want a pink Elise. I loved it and Guy has made some good sales on hot colours, but it's head over heart for the sensible businessman. 'When buying in used stock to sell, you want to go with something you can move on quickly rather than waiting for that one

Give me sunshine! Lotus designer Russell Carr's Elise S2 in a parade of Lotuses

person. Therefore shades of grey and blue might be perceived as fairly boring but it is what the majority of people go with.' So how do people react to the pink car? 'We had an open evening here for Evora and it had a steady stream of people looking at it, all making the same comment, "great car, love it, would never own it."' The bottom line is, if you are looking to preserve the car's value there's a lot to be said for demonstrating a bit of the herd instinct. When you are buying a new car, you will never see a return on £2000 ($3,000) for a premium paint colour, but if its pure head-turning pleasure you're after... go for it!

A similar rule applies to the interior. There are enough cars on the market to be choosy about trim. While you may be able to do without a radio because your Elise is all about the driving experience, that experience is enhanced by feeling cosseted in leather or alcantara upholstery. I prefer easing myself in and out of the Elise cockpit when the seat sides are leather rather than the strangely abrasive 'keprotec' (the brushed nylon material cladding standard seats), even though you can always fit aftermarket ones. Guy always specifies the Touring Pack, what used to be the Sport Tourer pack on the early S2s, for new cars that he orders for stock. His customers require it and on nearly new cars it is priced in – or not. So not having the touring pack devalues the car by the cost of the pack, and in the longer term hastens depreciation. It's worth having.

Personalising your car is part of pleasure of ownership, though one man's meat is another man's poison. Customising smacks of body-kits and may be a step too far. As Guy acknowledges, 'beauty is in the eye of the beholder. We've seen cars where people have applied so much chrome work, non-standard or different paint scheme, or put on too many stickers. I stand back and think, well, that's fine so long as you don't want to sell it, because it will be very difficult to find somebody else with similar tastes who'll accept it looking like that.'

NUMBER OF OWNERS

Guy is fairly tough on previous owner numbers. Recently he was offered a 5-owner, 55-plate Elise, just three-and-a-half years old. 'You've got to ask yourself,' he said, 'why has it gone through 5 owners in such a short time – more than one a year? And does that make it a good prospect when you want to sell it? The answer has to be "no". Whether it's a Series 1 from 1996 or a 111 R from 2009, he doesn't like to see more than 3 owners in total; after that, it starts to look suspicious. 'If a car has had 4 owners and you are buying as the fifth and selling onto the sixth, that's always going to be tough.'

EVIDENCE OF CRASH DAMAGE

Elise build quality is generally very good, especially that of Series 2 cars, so unless panel gaps are wildly out of true, you should be ok whatever model interests you. Anything cockeyed is indicative of a shunt or poor repair work. Avoid!

Elise 111R with the 1.8-litre Toyota engine, servicing access for essentials only!

SERVICE HISTORY

As a general rule, evidence of crash damage, number of owners, or lack of main dealer service history might put you off, but despite being a main dealer himself, with a natural desire to protect his exclusivity, Guy isn't totally averse to cars with the right kind of history. As he says 'There are plenty of people that declare themselves to be 'specialists', and obviously from a main dealer point of view I prefer to see main dealer service histories. But there are probably four or five UK specialists whose stamps I would be happy to see in a service book, who are actually more experienced and more enthusiastic than some main dealers. But when you are selling a car people expect it to match certain standards and that generally includes a main dealer service history.' That is especially so in its early years.

Plenty of miles on the clock may not be a disincentive – it's all about making a judgment on the service history and the way the car has been looked after by previous owners. Guy has just sold a 52,000 miles Elise S, a 2006 car that was serviced religiously every 9,000 miles, at 9, 18, 27, 36, and 45,000 miles. He describes it as 'the best driving Elise I have come across for ages, well used but not suffering at all.'

BUYING A CAR FOR TRACK DAYS

The rules can pretty much be thrown out if you are planning to buy a track day car. Guy says that there's an old trade saying – once a track car, always a track car; 'you can always tell. Generally it has got holes in it where the fire extinguisher was and where 4-point harnesses have been fitted, so if you are going to turn your pride-and-joy road car into a track car you will permanently diminish its value.' He often challenges people to come up with a good reason to modify a car for track day use by asking, 'do you want a track car for occasional

Has it been raced or rallied: At a check point on La Carrera Panamericana

road use or do you want a road car for occasional track use, because the Elise straight out of the box with no modifications like that is perfectly good for 6 track days a year, provided you don't mind not being the fastest thing out there.' Still, if you're out to win or set fastest time of day, the car has to evolve along track lines, and that means more power, harder suspension, different tyres and harder brake pads,

Having built the most successful S1 in the Lotus on Track Elise Trophy race series in 2008, Essex Autosport (formerly Sinclaire Motorsport) is ideally placed to provide sound counsel. I asked proprietor Wayne Sweeting what upgrades he'd advocate for the running gear for anyone heading for the track: 'there are brake upgrades, going from standard flexi-line to a braided steel line on the flexi-hose on the brakes. Running larger discs and obviously more aggressive (harder) pads than the road pad is quite common for upgrades. There's Nitron suspension too. These are all positive upgrades that will make the car's handling even better, more in line with what the car was designed for – a track car.' In Wayne's view that's what a true Elise is – a road-going track car, and from that perspective it can't be beat. 'After a day on track, other cars have worn their brakes out, got gear selection problems and

The interior of a Elise 111S with leather upholstery and touring pack

overheated, but these cars will run all day.'
In essence the better the car is on the track, the
worse it is on the road, and therefore the more
marginal its saleability. Guy's advice is to stick
with a road car unless you are a confirmed
track-day fiend. And in that case, break a few
purchasing rules: Go for a car with five owners,
with evidence of crash damage already,
because chances are you will add to it. Buy
cheaply so you've got a bit of money in the pot
to modify it to what you want.' It's more
economical to buy a car that's already been
modified than pay to have the work done,
though doing it yourself brings discounts. Same
goes for restorations: you never recover the
outlay of having the work done, so let someone
else take the hit unless you love getting down
and dirty with the socket set and the fibreglass
resin. If you're going to hang on to the car, keep
on top of bodywork and mechanical issues as
and when they occur so it doesn't degenerate
into a shed.

The best way to put value into a race car is to
win – then people want it alright. But Guy's view
is that, 'on a typical grid of 26 cars there are 25
people who have devalued their car completely
and one who is keeping its value up by winning.'
Still, if you yearn for the thrill of the chase, that
might outweigh mundane resale considerations!

LEFT-HAND DRIVE VERSUS RIGHT-HAND DRIVE

There are several world markets where traffic
drives on the left side of the road and currency
fluctuations sometime make importing cars from
right-side driving nations attractive. Doing this
may make sense for the Ferrari and Porsche
market, but the Elise is lower down the price
index than the average supercar. There's little
obvious benefit. Series 1 cars are easy to
convert from left to right and back again, but
Series 2 models are more complicated, and
post-2006 models are virtually impossible. Guy
Munday's opinion is to question why anybody

should spend (say) £9k on a left-hand drive car and have to sit on the wrong side of the road, when you can buy a decent Series 2 for between £12 and £14k? However if you split your driving between the two different traffic flows (as with the UK and mainland Europe), it might be worthwhile.

MODIFIED CARS

Elise fans questing performance advantage have tried installing an assortment of replacement engines including the Honda K20A Type R iVTEC engine, or even the four-cylinder unit from the Suzuki Hayabusa GSX1300R, the world's fastest production motorcycle. The 2.3-litre Ford Duratec is another, less frenetic alternative, and I've also seen the Audi TT's 1.8t 20V turbo unit installed. There are a few V6 Audi 3.2s out there too, beautifully fitted, delivering 300bhp (220kW) with brakes to match, but still an unknown quantity. An alarming prospect, some might say. But for sure, the prospect of obtaining 0-60mph in 4.0sec and 0-100mph in 9.5sec by straight-swapping a 220bhp (161kW) six-speed Honda powertrain makes the standard Rover K-series seem quite prosaic. But

this is a twilight world where boy racer meets hot-rodder and there's an element of make-do and mend which pros like Guy Munday steer well clear of. 'It confounds me that people want to modify cars to that extent,' he comments. 'Visit all the forums and there are 101 different opinions on the suitability of various tyres, dampers and brakes. When you consider that Lotus are one of the world's foremost ride and handling consultants to the whole motor industry, and the Elise is the shop window for what they do, why people need to keep mucking around with them I don't know. The car is brilliant out of the box.' If there's a genuine reason for keeping an old Lotus on the road – say, it's K-series head-gasket has gone, or if you are the type who enjoys being a home mechanic, it might make sense, but ask yourself the question: for several thousand pounds installing a different engine, why not just buy a newer car? Cars do come up that have been fitted with an aftermarket turbo – like Turbo Tecnics. Now Lotus is supercharging Elise and Exige, not to mention the Europa S turbo, surely there's a case to be made? Not in Guy's book. 'We have actually put a few of those right for people,' he

Elise SC with its ex-factory super-charged Toyota engine

Elise S1 front suspension: Bilsteins are a favoured replacement for the original Koni dampers

Elise S1: Factory spec parts and set up avoids warranty claim hassles

Production assembly of brake systems

says. 'The K-series engines aren't designed for that sort of forced induction and the level of power it creates. Again, if you spend £6- 8k on a conversion you may as well buy yourself a later car with a more powerful engine anyway.'

I asked Wayne Sweeting of Essex Autosport about the enhancements that he thinks are worth making to an Elise. 'The most popular aftermarket engine management system for the S1's K-series is the Emerald K3 system, which affords full remapping capabilities as well as its own data-logging options through the software it comes with,' he tells me. 'It's able to control a number of auxiliary devices as well as accept input from 0-5v Analogue output-equipped wideband lambda systems. Emerald is a fantastically simple and effective engine management system that can grow with your car's power output.'

Wayne isn't altogether averse to the Turbo Tecnics supercharger on the K-series engine, but it was overtaken by installing a Honda Type-R engine or the Ford Duratec unit instead, as he says, 'because they were less stressed and they dropped in the Elise engine bay straight out of the box from the manufacturers.

The engine mounting points in the chassis didn't need adjusting because you had a conversion plate.' Bumping up the Honda Type-R with a supercharger sends a mighty 300bhp through the wheels, and the 2.0-litre unit is a stronger engine than the 1800 K-series, so runs rings round it on the circuit. From 2010 non-standard engines were not allowed in the Elise Trophy series; they have to be original equipment production engines, either the K-series or Toyota, in supercharged and normally aspirated format, with different categories for both versions.

The Series 1 is well served for induction kits, with systems available from Hurricane, ITG and K&N. As Wayne points out, 'it's not limited to simple airbox designs though; the S1 can also be easily fitted with Jenvey throttle bodies which offer significant power gains.' For the ultimate normally-aspirated applications, camshafts ranging from mild to wild are available for the Rover K-series, and when matched to a gas-flowed cylinder head, the K-series can produce around 200bhp (147kW).

For upgraded exhaust systems Wayne recommends Janspeed. 'They are excellent quality and well priced,' he says. 'For application on the Elise S1 they bring mild power gains alone, but coupled with a good induction system and re-mappable engine management, they give significant improvements. Also proven to work well on the S1 Elise is the tubular back-box, which can be bought with a range of different tailpipes.'

How about suspension upgrades? 'Nitron dampers are the optimum solution for all road and track applications,' according to Wayne Sweeting, 'and they can be tailored to suit both car and driver.' Nitron supply dampers in three basic configurations: for fast road and track use, the Nitron 1-Way is ideal, with a single adjustment control on the damper tube which controls bump and rebound in equal measure. For a heavier track bias the Nitron 2-Way, features a remote reservoir that houses a bump adjustment control, while the damper tube adjustment controls rebound. For the ultimate track and race applications there is the Nitron 3-Way damper, which again features a remote reservoir with adjustment of both fast and slow bump, while rebound is again to be found on the damper tube.' Lower cost alternatives to Nitron are GAZ dampers. 'For our main road and light track applications we recommend GAZ 1-Way dampers, with adjustment for bump and rebound handled by one control.' Wayne favours Bilsteins as a damper replacement. 'S2 Bilstein dampers are a common and cost-effective upgrade for the Series 1,' he says. 'This option is a complete kit including dampers, springs and updated mounting brackets and it's a very popular upgrade that transforms the handling of the S1. It eliminates most of the knocks and rattles associated with the Elise S1 suspension.' On brakes, Wayne advises that, 'AP Racing's 4-piston conversion is by far the best brake upgrade available for the Elise S1. It includes fitting AP Racing 4-piston front calipers, and optionally uprating the rear calipers, giving the most devastating stopping power. It's what we use on our race winning Elise S1.' This conversion incorporates braided brake lines all round, which improve pedal feel and are better made than standard brake lines. The final part of this conversion is an uprated master cylinder, which moves a greater volume of fluid than the standard master cylinder and allows for greater clamping load at the brakes for any given amount of pedal pressure. Pagid RS42 brake pads are available for road and track, or the more aggressive RS14, which is a dedicated track day and race brake pad. All Pagid pads provide superb stopping power, excellent fade resistance and they are nonasbestos. An often-overlooked part of the braking system is the brake fluid itself and for all road and track applications Essex Autosport recommend Castrol SRF because it offers the most consistent braking performance under all temperature conditions. Photo Brake disc & chassis...

NON-STANDARD AND REPLACEMENT COMPONENTS

Much depends on the age of the car you're buying whether or not you suggest factory or pattern or aftermarket parts. Elise Parts (www.eliseparts.com), founded by Geary Powell, offers a vast selection of components and equipment for the Elise: from body panels and parts to drivelines and running gear, it's all obtainable on-line or direct from their Cambridgeshire, UK premises.

Keeping to the book, Guy Munday prefers everything on his cars to be of Lotus manufacture, be it sports exhaust or wheels, because he wants to be certain that components have undergone the Lotus testing and validation process in order to protect the car's warranty, and in some cases, ensuring the car passess the annual roadworthiness check. Generally main dealers favour cars in standard trim as it's

the lowest risk position in terms of sustaining a good reputation for probity and protecting their warranty offer. Other dealers do trade in tuned cars, with brake and engine conversion kits and sports exhausts, but remember that the long-term impact of these mods on the whole car is untried.

Suspension components on all Elises are robust, though upgrades are not uncommon. Stratton Motor Company's service department maintains plenty of early cars, and Guy keeps a weather eye on wear and tear. Like Wayne Sweeting, he goes with Bilsteins to replace Series 1 Konis, and finds Series 2 suspension quite acceptable under a Series 1. The early cars had MMC brakes (sand cast metal matrix discs), which are now almost obsolete, so they have almost all been replaced with conventional cast iron components.

WHEELS

Over the years Lotus hasn't offered that many wheel options on Elises. The standard issue alloy is a five-spoke star pattern with slashes along each arm towards the wheel rim, four bolt holes and Lotus logo hub cap at centre. A new six-spoke design replaced this in May 1999, which was similar to the 340R without the split-

Standard alloy wheel for the 2009 Elise SC

Original alloy wheel on the Elise S1

rim sophistication. The original wheel was painted gold on the 50th anniversary edition, and the 111S went to a plainer six-spoke wheel. In February 2000 the Sport 160 model was equipped with a smart unfussy five-spoke wheel, spokes tapering slightly towards the rim. Modern cars have two wheel options, the forged one being lighter than the cast option, which gives the choice of forged alloys as part of the sport pack. For 2011, a set of new Lotus Elise forged wheels weighed 29.26kg (64.5lbs) per set, 2.14kg (4.7lbs) lighter than a set of lightweight cast versions.

Once you move into the zone of different-sized aftermarket wheels you are in murky waters and could upset the work that Lotus has done to get the car right in the first place. It wouldn't impress Guy Munday either: 'if a car were presented with the wrong size, wrong design wheels I would think twice about it. An upgrade like Sport 160 Dymag or 111S wheels on a standard car is perfectly acceptable. That said, a standard S1 wheel weighs 6.8kg (15lbs) and ironically a Motorsport wheel is a few pounds heavier.' Magnesium Dymag, OZ or Speedline weigh roughly 4kg (9lb) each so it's clear that fitting aftermarket wheels is a simple way of reducing weight. Expect to pay £1,000- £1,500 (US$1500-$2250) a set and include a hub fitting kit too. Another make of aftermarket wheel, Rota, is much cheaper (£500/US$750 a set) and available for the Series 1 Elise. These are 5-spoke and finished in gunmetal or matt black. Nothing short of a stripe over the top of the car affects its look more than a set of wheels and a set of black alloys gives any Elise a racier image.

TYRES

Tyres have moved on a long way in 15 years and the original Pirelli P-Zeros (front 185/55 R15, rear 205/50 R16) used on the Series 1 are no longer available so most owners fit the factory approved Yokohama Advan Neova LTS equivalent. Out in clubland there are differing views on what gives the best possible results; Michelin Pilot SXs, Dunlop D98s and Toyo Proxes are workable options, though they go off quickly. The company approved Yokohama C-Drive (185/55 front, 205/50 rear) have more conventional tread and are thus more suitable for S1 winter use.

Series 2s used to be fitted with Bridgestone Potenza RE040s (175/55R16 front and 225/45R17 rear) and they suited the car very well. At 2010, Elise tyre of choice was the Yokohama Advan Neova AD07 LTS, 175/50 R16 front and 225/45 R17 rear. A drive story to Geneva, Morzine, Chamonix (in Switzerland) and the ice-racing stadium at Serre Chevalier last winter demonstrated how well winter tyres serve you in the snow. The Lotuses were shod with Yokohama W*Drive winter tyres and Pirelli Sottozero studded tyres for the labyrinth of the Andros Trophy's ice rink and were sure-footed and utterly unshakable. Everyone should have spare set of wheels shod with winter tyres, ready to go when the white stuff dumps on us!

GOING TOPLESS

So you're buying a sports car? That's wind in the hair motoring you're after then? Well, on a hot day in St Tropez, topless is matchless, but the crucial convertible conundrum is not how good it feels with the top down, but how well it works with the top on, when it's raining and when your passenger is, shall we say, keener on comfort than carburettors. Guy Munday knows his way around an Elise roofline, and he is realistic: 'I would never declare an early Elise to be completely waterproof, though later ones probably are.'

The fundamental cause of water coming in is seldom the hood itself, it's more likely to be a problem with the fine adjustment of its fitting,

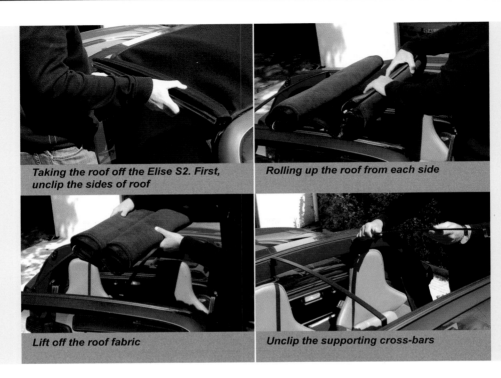

Taking the roof off the Elise S2. First, unclip the sides of roof

Rolling up the roof from each side

Lift off the roof fabric

Unclip the supporting cross-bars

though a water repellent coating on the soft top will improve the hood's resistance to leaks. Even if you get the fitting perfectly correct, you can still expect a few drips on the sill when you open the door after it's been standing out on a rainy night. The Elise soft top is not a quick bit of kit to erect, however. To do it at a leisurely pace can take maybe five minutes, so there's none of that 'up and down at the traffic lights' stuff. It's easier to describe how to assemble the hood than how to take it down. So here goes: assuming you've started with the top off, to put it up you first need to locate the cant rails that pass down either side, between roll hoop and A-pillar, just above the side windows. These cant rails are tapered towards the front, and have a ball fitting that pops into the windscreen header rail, while the back end has a neat little clip.

You hold the cant rail and apply a little bit of

pressure by leaning into the windscreen and the clip at the rear fits into its housing on the door shut. The cant rails are braced by two virtually flat hoops that pass from side to side across the car and they spring-fit into place.

You take the hood itself and cast it over the lattice frame you've just created. A plastic fillet runs along the leading edge of the hood and you slide that under the ridge along the length of the windscreen header rail. It's best to start with the corner sections, which are separated from the major part of it.

When you are satisfied that the front is flush, you can pop the chrome spikes at the rear into the receptacles provided in the flying buttresses. At the sides, poppers press on to fixings in the cant rails inside the cockpit. Finally, you return to the rear and tension the whole canopy by means of a pair of Allen bolts set in the spikes

Each cross-bar attaches in a slot at the top of the windscreen

Refitting: with the cross-bars installed, stretch the roof across the cross-bars

It's important to slot the two side pins into the windscreen top rail

Positioning the side rails to complete the roof refitting. It takes just minutes!

using the Allen key provided. This little tool has a home in the rear bulkhead just behind the driver's seat.

If you plan to use the car all year round or if you prefer the coupé shape or security of a firm lid, you can fit a works GRP hardtop and transform the Elise into a coupé. Guy Munday believes it's not a vital necessity: 'if it's for better weather protection, don't bother, because the soft top is fine, especially on modern cars. If it's about noise reduction, a hardtop doesn't make any difference. But if you need it for everyday railway parking or on street parking, the security case makes it worth it.'

All Elise hardtops are removable, so if you go to view a prospective car with the roof on, bear in mind that the standard car has a soft-top anyway, ready to go on if you need it.

ECONOMY

There is an increasing trend for buyers to focus on CO_2 readings and fuel consumption rather than out-and-out performance stats, though if you enjoy a blast that's the kind of downer data you'd rather not know about. If you want economy, go buy a tdi!

However, cost-per-mile, the Elise runs cheaper than a 2.0-litre Mondeo, so it's a no-brainer for petrolheads with enlightened company car policies. Now that company car taxation is related to lower emission figures, the Elise is beginning to be attractive to fleet buyers and leasing companies. Although Guy sells 90 per cent of his stock for private recreational use, this area is growing especially for young professionals in modern businesses where the Elise is a genuine alternative to a mainstream model.

The car that you're viewing looks pristine, superficially. But what sort of life has it led? Are there gremlins lurking within that polished plastic exterior? I've asked a couple of well-known Lotus experts to help guide us through the pitfalls and legacies of Elise construction and design. Though Guy Munday generally deals with more recent Elises at Stratton Motor Company his expertise frequently takes him back in time and, having a long career history with the marque, he has a profound grasp of issues that have affected the cars over the years. That's essential ground for enthusiastic punters and Guy talked me though concerns that are known to affect Elises. As he says, although there are a number of problems with earlier cars, most of which have been ironed out at the factory as the model evolved, Elises are far from disaster prone and there are fixes and repairs on tap to cure most glitches.

For a second opinion I've travelled to Martlesham near Ipswich, Suffolk, to see Greg Lock whose business is called Hangar 111. He specialises in Elises, Exiges and the minimalist KTM X-Bow slingshot and he has a fund of knowledge borne of hard-won experience on all ages of Elise and Exige. I also find he and his wife Marianne owned the orange Elise that graces the cover of my book on the Series 1 Elise published back in 1998. When I call, he's working on an S2 with a blowing flexi-section in the exhaust. It is a common occurrence and it rubs on the undertray making a terrible polystyrene chaffing noise. It also has a rattling driver's window and knocking rear suspension caused by worn ball joints. There's a heady mix of S1, S2 road and race cars in the workshop, and a very tasty, fully-spec'ed Exige 320 receiving the very latest bodywork evolutions. Generally, Greg prefers not to have too many projects on the go so he and his engineer Rob can devote their energies to one car at a time.

The Elise 111 engine bay

The Gold Leaf Team Lotus commemorative edition of the Elise S1

We'll hear Greg's observations and advice, along with Guy's, as we look in more detail at the Elise constituent parts.

Elise Series 1

CHASSIS AND BODYWORK

From the outset, Guy is upbeat. Not only is he constantly monitoring Lotus's build quality, he's also abreast of solutions to customers' Elise problems, both S1 and S2. 'From Series 1 through to the early Series 2s, they tend to suffer from the same issues,' he says. 'To start with, if you get one up on a ramp you look for floor damage under the car – the main central tub – and if someone's driven over a boulder or it's been jacked up in the wrong place it may have creased the floor plan. Someone may have jacked it up within the frame, where it is only a 2mm skin, and we have seen areas where somebody has put a jack onto the soft floor panel rather than the structural area.' Check the undertray at the rear to see if the car's been

jacked up at the back. 'Under a wheel area they sometimes don't understand there's a soft skin underneath. It's just an aluminium panel to take the air ducting through the car and jacking it up there will obviously distort the panel.'

Guy flags up the floorpan corrosion issue. 'The S1's footwell mat is not a carpet, it's a hard, plastic mat bonded onto the aluminium to give you some tread-plate area. If it's lumpy, that could denote corrosion beneath it on the floor panel – if the car leaks and moisture ends up on the floor, it creeps under this bonded mat to the floor surface. There is a treatment: remove the mat and neutralise the corrosion with a special neutralising wash available from Lotus dealerships.'

It's all down to how the car has been stored. Garaged, there's unlikely to be a problem, but a car that spends the winter outside, even if it is well looked after, will be at risk. As Guy says, 'If you're going to buy a nice car you don't want to see a big corrosion issue. So neutralise it. Put a nice set of rubber mats down which can be

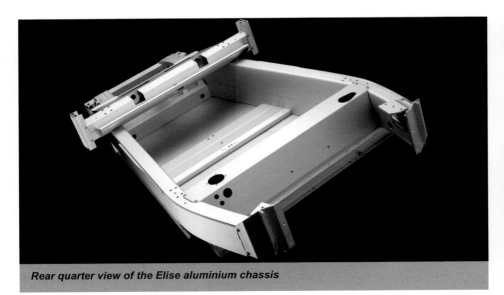

Rear quarter view of the Elise aluminium chassis

controlled to make sure the moisture can't attack the metal.'

It's not like you are going to see daylight through the floor, though. Greg has only ever seen one car, 'with a fingernail-sized hole in the floor, due to the way the aluminium anodises and frosts up. It's not structural; it's just the floor-pan. So the fix is a new aluminium sheet on the floor and the mat goes over the top.' The S2 doesn't suffer the same mats problem because the carpet is not bonded, though Greg has come across owners who've installed aftermarket rubber mats simply to catch shoe dirt, and these harbour condensation beneath them.

When motoring long distances, the side of the chassis can get quite warm, as I found on the run from Lotus USA's offices in Atlanta, Georgia, down to Daytona, Florida. It wasn't as if I was wearing shorts even, and as it got hotter so I was aware of my left shin gently roasting. It is just a feature of the car, and it's because aluminium water-pipes run down the inside of the chassis side members from front radiator to rear engine. Such contrasts in temperatures can play a part in setting off corrosion, as Greg points out: 'we have seen a few Series 1 cars where there's a corroded floor-pan under the floor-mat, but nothing as severe as rumour suggests. Though we have seen two examples that have been repaired by what appears to be a sheet of aluminium bonded over the top of the footwell space,' he laughs. 'I once spent an hour in the foot-wells of a French customer's car removing the aluminium oxide powder from the surface of the foot-well floors.

There weren't any holes in that one, but you can see how the problem might escalate. In my opinion, the root cause seems to be from the original grey 'knobbly' rubber mats that were glued into the foot-wells on early cars. The contrasting heat and cold in the foot-wells meant condensation built up here.'

Corrosion can occur where steel meets aluminium

Corrosion on chassis external mounting point

Corrosion visible in this footwell

ROOF

Greg advocates prevention rather than cure for leaking roofs: 'we always suggest to customers to use a shower cape over the roof area to minimise it dripping through the doors into the cabin area and onto your chair.' He's averse to full covers because they can generate corrosion, but one that goes over the roof area and either side of the drop windows, down the front screen and over the back area is satisfactory.

PAINT FINISH

All cars suffer from stone chips and the Elise is no exception. 'There's usually heavy stone chipping to the front because of its design,' says Guy. 'It's a very low car and it takes the hits.' You can apply protection film, Armafend and Ventureshield, to the front and sides. These Transparent plastic sheets are now fitted as standard around the nose of the car and leading edge of the rear wheel arches, and headlight covers (for S1s) are also smart as well as practical.

One of the telltale signs of a car that's lived hard on the track is that most of the paint will be missing around the inside of the rear wheelarches. 'The trailing edge of the wheelarches will end up frayed because of the stones hitting them,' says Greg. 'We put Armafend or clear film over the corners and that protects it but otherwise there's no cure apart from a ghastly looking mud flap. Glass-fibre is a problem in general for stone chips,' he says. 'The flexible nature of the material means that even the best paint, the most expensive clear film and other treatments simply won't stop the damage. Basically when a stone hits the glass-fibre there is a tiny flex in the surface that detaches the paint. This will happen even underneath clear protection film. Track day cars suffer around the rear flanks just ahead of the rear wheels because of the sideways motion, and though the clear film can delay the process, eventually the paint flakes off in this area, along with the film. Semi-slick tyres increase stone chips down the sides, including the doors and especially around the underside of the door handle. Repair is dependent on the severity of the damage. Small ones are easy to remove with a touch-up stick, credit card, a soft cloth and T-cut.'

It's not just the bodywork that's vulnerable: the front and rear grilles are prone to stone damage

Rear view of the Elise S1. A shower cape will help keep wetness out when standing

Elise S1, detail of headlight nascelles, indicators and driving lamps

and rust, and the remedy is to have them powder-coated and re-finished. Paint can crack and flake at the left rear of the car due to the close proximity of the hot exhaust. In 2000 there were issues with yellow and orange pigments and the factory delayed production of cars ordered in these colours until the problems were sorted out. Yellow was back on the menu from June 2001, though if contemplating a car from these years and in either of those colours it makes sense to examine the finish carefully. If buying from a dealer ask for a pot of the appropriate touch-up paint or order one up yourself.

LOOSE HEADLIGHTS

It's easy to check that the headlights are secure. Guy explains: 'on the S1's headlights with the 7.5-inch lens, if they haven't got their covers on, the customer should give the headlight a gentle push to make sure that they are still bonded correctly. The location brackets that are bonded to the front clam can corrode, so the bonding material is stuck to the surface of the clams which then flake away and that starts to cause floppy headlights.' If you are driving along and

Inevitable stone chipping to the frontal area

Clear film helps protect the wheelarch fronts

S1 headlights can get 'floppy'

Paint flaking behind the rear grilles

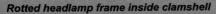
Rotted headlamp frame inside clamshell

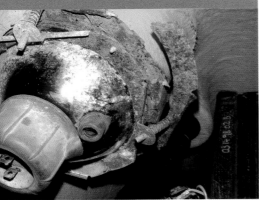
Headlamp collapsed inside the cover

Rear view of a collapsed headlamp frame

see your lights flickering up and down, this is probably the cause. The front turn signal lamps can fall out, flailing around on the end of their cables and damaging the front clamshell.

'Loose headlights are due to corroded location brackets,' confirms Greg. 'The original bracket is made from zinc-passivated steel, and water will eventually push past the flimsy – badly designed – rubber seal around the lamp bowl and soak the brackets. Couple that with the often-missing bulb-access-hole bung from the wheel arch liner and you have a recipe for rotting headlamp brackets and bowls alike.' The problem can be sorted by replacement clams or replacement mounting brackets, which is a relatively big deal.

HEADLIGHT COVERS

The Series 1 Elise was originally supplied with headlight covers that had a tedious tendency to steam up and distort the light beam. Lotus failed to find a solution to this and the car was then supplied without them. Later variants like the 111S were delivered with them as standard but the misting up problem was never fully resolved. You can even see it happening in modern Lotuses like the Europa and Evora.

Greg explains: 'Steamed-up headlight covers on 111S model are purely down to the nature of the beast,' he points out. 'This is what happens when the flimsy rubber seal and the 111S plastic headlamp cover are not well seated and therefore not sealed properly. Additionally, the headlamp cowling – bonded to the clamshell as a separate part – can have air gaps in the bonded faces, thus creating a place for moisture to sit - especially after washing. Just add a northern hemisphere summer and you have condensation - a bit like cheap double glazing!'

BODYWORK FIXINGS

The inner wheelarch liners are fastened to the

underside of the wings by Phillips screws. These are zinc-plated steel – galvanized in other words – but they can corrode which makes undoing them difficult. Best replace with stainless steel ones when the car's on a hoist.

FRONT AND REAR COMPARTMENT RELEASE CABLES

If the boot (trunk) release is stiff it could be because the lubrication originally applied on the production line wasn't quite adequate. The dealer should have picked this up at the pre-delivery inspection, but fresh oiling and greasing will sort it out. The same is true of the bonnet (hood) release mechanism, though that may be down to one or two other issues. The pin and catch could be out of alignment and need specialist attention to re-align. As a temporary measure, take hold of the bonnet at its rear edge up by the screen and try moving it from side to side while exerting upward pressure. You can also try pushing the bonnet shut while a friend pulls the handle, which, if it's successful, is an indication that the catch needs lubricating. If all else fails the catch is accessible through the wheel arch liner, though not an easy operation.

SIDE WINDOWS

'You want to see good operation of the drop glass side windows,' says Greg. 'We're talking window winders (lifters). On the rubber-backed tracks or the channels that hold the glass pane, it's common for the felt to be worn into the channels, especially on the driver's side.' It's a knock-on effect - the felt surface normally has a smooth action on the window, but once that felt is worn away from the inside edge, the window tends to grip on the rubber backing. If that's not regularly lubricated, the window can be stiff to operate up or down, which blows the bonded clips from the window. Then, Greg tells me, 'the window just drops like a guillotine and it's a glass replacement job, or at least re-bonding of replacement clips, and that's a couple of hours work to deal with the door and tracks again. If you're replacing the rubber backed tracks and a door glass repair, that's a good morning's work. It's not common, just wear and tear but in an 8-year old car you would look for it.'

As Greg says, it's a more common occurrence than you'd expect: 'windows that have fallen off of their runners due to bonded clips coming off is a result of other problems,' he

Stiff window lifters can mean replacement tracks – potentially a long job

tells me, 'and I have done 100s of these! It is the dryness of the felt channels that causes the window to bind and the user to force the mechanism. The glue gets dry and brittle over time and the force from the user cracks the glue holding the plastic clip to the glass.'

The other blemish that occurs is that the black weather strip that runs along the door top and keeps water from going between window and door can become distorted over time, and simply needs replacing.

DOOR MIRRORS

Sourced from the Rover Metro parts bin, the door-mounted mirrors are apt to loose their settings to the extent of drooping. This frustrating quirk is due to the smoothness of the ball-joint they swivel on. A Do-It-Yourself solution is to abrade the ball with file or sandpaper and retighten. More seriously, stress fractures in the plastic mounting plate can cause the mirror to work loose, resulting in a gap between the unit's painted arm and the black joint from which it pivots. The mirror assembly is secured by a single screw so an eye needs to be kept on it and is a point worth checking before purchase.

But as Guy points out, 'it's not massively common. It depends on how critical you want to be. If they're loose, the mirror head needs replacement, and that's not a Lotus issue because it's an old British Leyland product. It's not to do with the mounting of it; it's the head unit itself. The spring within the head becomes weak and at high speed the mirrors can fold in.'

Greg has a fix: 'The ball-joint in the mirror housing is prone to becoming 'smooth',' he says. 'You can almost bet that the cars where this happened were used by multiple drivers, each moving the mirror for their own height and also rotating it to make it easier when parking kerb-side. I've never been aware of an actual design defect that causes this. The best way to resolve it was to replace that part of the housing, and our 'DIY' fix for this is fairly simple - expose the ball-joint and very carefully wipe a smear of superglue across the surface of the ball and allow to dry. This roughens and thickens the surface of the ball therefore giving it back its mojo.'

DOOR RETAINERS

Door retainers could sometimes snap on early

The S1 exterior mirror pivot can wear, but there are simple fixes

Using the wrong coolant causes deposits in pipes leading to overheating

This old style coolant reservoir has cracked and been repaired poorly

New style replacement coolant reservoir is less prone to breakage

cars, involving the loss of a 125mm (5in) section of aluminium. The fix cost £80 ($120) and took an hour to achieve, though happily the relevant front clam did not need removing. The design was subsequently improved.

COOLANT SYSTEM

Aluminium radiators are always recommended by the independents. As Greg explains, 'it's fully welded, instead of the plastic tank originals that can cause an issue if the engine or your system is pressurised or goes over pressure – the softest area within that is the tanks on the side of the radiators. It's quite common for us it to suggest a fully-welded tanked radiator to eliminate that weak area.' Radiator leaks can be spotted from the tank side. The jubilee clips on the radiator hoses need to be checked regularly to make sure there's no loss of coolant.

The coolant bottle can crack or split with time. Replacement is the only remedy.

HOT FLUSH

On older S1 Elises there was a problem with the clutch's 'red' hydraulic hose. This ran from the master cylinder at the pedal box to the slave cylinder attached to the clutch in the engine bay,

via the radiator return pipe to which it was strapped in the front of the car. Engine and radiator heat combined to soften the hydraulic hose so that pedal effort went into expanding the pipe and not in moving the clutch plates, which made gear changes difficult. Re-routing the hose improved the situation, but there was no substitute for a steel braided hose, a remedy applied to all new Elises. Also, the slave cylinder fixing plate is also susceptible to engine-bay temperatures and can flex, leading to problems with gearshifts.

FAN CLUB

It's worth checking the radiator fan to make sure it works. Have the engine running at normal temperatures. Because the radiator is flat, water runs through it and straight into the fan unit motor. First sign of trouble is a noisy fan. Problems tend to show up in the spring: if the car's not used for 3 or 4 months, or during the winter when the fan will probably never come on – around May there can be an issue. You're in the traffic on a warm day and all of a sudden you've got 102 flashing on your dash and your fan hasn't worked. It's not common, but it is worth checking that it's got a fan control and that it's working correctly. When it comes on the water temperature should drop and it's controlled.

The S2's coolant temperatures rise much higher than the S1, as high as 107°C. While the S2 shop manual rates this as perfectly normal, the standard S1's normal working temperature is 87°C, which can drop to 84°C on the motorway with better airflow over the radiator. The S1 fan activates at 100°C, when the readout begins to flash, going off again once it's dropped to 93°C. The S2's pressurized system means it will not actually boil until 120°C is reached.

There is another point: if an S1 appears to be running 20°C below its normal operating temperature it means the thermostat has probably failed. Unless you stop, the temperature reading will eventually return to normal and the head-gasket will blow.

INTERIOR
SEATS

The Series 1s had a little black squeezy pump like the doctor takes your blood pressure with, down beside your left hip, with which you could inflate the backrest to provide more or less lumbar support. Its purpose is to increase or deflate the seat back pressure while in motion, in order to achieve top comfort. I came to the conclusion that the seat still lacked under-thigh support and in an ideal world I would probably fit a seat with a longer squab and a bit more stuffing.

STEERING AND SUSPENSION

Listen out for a repetitive bumping or rumbling noise when the car's going along as it probably indicates that a wheel bearing needs replacement. With regard to the steering, rack play can be an issue: 'they are very delicate pieces of machinery,' Guy points out, 'so a good thump down a pothole can cause damage to suspension arms or the delicate rack. It's a very precise movement; as soon as you go from steering column to one UJ it's straight to your rack so you get very positive feel back, and you can feel these issues as they occur.'

Dampers (shock absorbers) are a regular

Elementary cockpit of the S1 Gold Leaf Team Lotus edition

Early stage corrosion visible on the lower rear wishbone mountings

replacement part. 'Lots of the early cars are on the original red Koni shocks,' says Guy, 'and if you've gone over a bump there will be a very hard clunk from the suspension. Most people move onto Bilstein or Nitron, Gaz or Spax – they all make a kit for the Lotus Elise.' Indeed, the straightforward replacement for S1's Koni dampers is a set of S2 Bilsteins. It consists of four dampers, four springs and a pair of brackets for the rear, and is a winning recipe all round. According to Greg, 'it imparts a refined feel because the suspension becomes silent, it's about 20 per cent stiffer than standard and it lowers the car by about 10mm (0.4in) all round to give a 130mm (5.1in) ride height. It feels really nice on the road, and it livens the car up a lot.'

The valving on the Bilstein damper is so much smoother to the extent that you can have a virtually silent drive; there's no knocking or crashing of the suspension as there was with the original S1. Everything is made to a price, and when the S2 came out it was designed to

This upper wishbone is in poor condition

Surface corrosion on suspension member

S2's Bilsteins replace S1's Konis

be a more refined car and hence was equipped with uprated suspension. Design of the S2 wishbones was slightly different, giving a slightly wider track and the wishbones were re-enforced, though the suspension design and layout was identical conceptually so the cars could be set up equally as capable as each other. The Bilstein kit costs £600 ($900), so when the Konis are worn out it's the way to go. As Greg says, 'with a full geometry overhaul and a set of Bilsteins on an aging S1 it actually feels like a new car to drive. It's easy to forget just how old the S1 is now. By contrast with the modern Elise, Exige and Europa it's almost like they've gone too far and they are overly refined for the purpose they were intended.'

Check the anti-roll bar fitting as well. 'In a perfect motor sport world, using solid nylon blocks for the anti-roll bar was the more purist way for it to be done,' says Greg. 'The downside was a creak at the front as the anti roll bar was loaded, and it would creak within the nylon block. When servicing early cars we drop the block and use a white grease or a copper slip to

lubricate the tube between and try to stop the creaking.' Lotus updated them from about '98 to a rubber-based clamp, which eliminated that problem. And don't forget to see if the car has been jacked up on its wishbones by mistake, because they will be bent as a consequence.

Damaged suspension arms can even be due to excessive sliding around roundabouts, and dropping off kerbs with a clunk. The obvious cause, then, is impact damage, leading to bent arms or tie-rods. Greg describes a few of the issues: 'Damaged rear tie rods are often bent by tyre fitters who aren't knowledgeable or experienced with the cars – we fit our own tyres here at Hangar 111 just to be sure. A damaged tie-rod messes up the handling and means a new rod is required to get things back in spec. It's not detrimental to the value of the car if resolved, though.'

When the car's up on the ramp you can give the suspension a once over, and it's then that the extent of corrosion on wishbones and suspension components becomes apparent. However it's not necessarily catastrophic. For instance you often see corrosion on the stabiliser on the right rear, though Greg says it's rarely an issue: 'Worst case is it will crack, and that's usually down to poor clutch control and stabbed gear changes, but they're quite easy to replace.'

Bent wishbones: 'accident damage can leave wishbones bent and thus give you poor suspension alignment – unless masses of spacer shims are used to correct the suspension (watch out for this – if a car has what seems like a lot of shims in the suspension, check the wishbones). Worst case is where a wishbone has stood up to the impact and the chassis has become bent. Anything that looks odd in that area – avoid.'

Rusty suspension arms: 'they tend to look worse than they really are, but this will become an issue in future. The original zinc-passivate coating will keep working (providing nobody sands off the rust!) but will become chipped and scratched over time. We blast them, examine and then stove-bake-enamel the wishbones to ensure good life-span. It is inexpensive compared to a new set of wishbones.'

ENGINE AND GEARBOX
HEAD-GASKET FAILURE IN THE ROVER K-SERIES ENGINE

The Series 1's Rover K-series driveline is broadly reliable but it has gained a reputation for head-gasket failure. The gasket material is not as good as it might be, and the malfunction generally occurs over a 6mm (0.24in) surface area on the cylinder head between water jacket and outer face, causing the seal bonded to the steel gasket to blow, with the accompanying water leak.

Modifications were made to the K-series unit in 2001 which alleviated the problem by improving the alignment between head-gasket and engine block, as well as altering the gasket for better sealing and oil drain-back, so in principle post-2001 engines should be less prone to failure. In fact Guy thinks failure is pretty random, though he tends to stay away from Rover-engined cars now that they are at the least 6 and at the most 15-years old. As he says, 'we had to do one on a 20,000-mile Series 1 recently, while one of lads here (at Stratton Motor Co) has a 105,000-miler that has never blown a head-gasket. The only thing I would say that is if the head-gasket does go, it won't go a second time because when you replace it you'll fit upgraded bits. So the general advice is if you are going to buy a Rover-powered car that hasn't had its head gasket done, it's well to budget for this just in case.'

Once Ford had taken Rover over and dealt with the Land Rover Freelander head-gasket

Surface rusting visible on this top wishbone

Tell-tale signs of a blown K-Series head gasket

Measuring the depth of the cylinder liners after K-series engine head gasket failure

issues, the latest generation of gaskets was fine. So if one has been replaced the problem doesn't tend to return, unless there's an issue with the head. The head could have become porous or distorted. In normal cases it's pressure-tested and skimmed to get a correct, flat surface. The magic mileage is between 30-40k: if it's going to go it will be around there. So perhaps if a K-series car makes it over 40k it will be all right.

At the other end of the scale, the fuel injection pump fuse can blow, consigning you to the tender mercies of a roadside recovery, all for want of a part worth a few pennies. The original 10amp fuse became a 20amp fuse on later cars, and it's prudent to carry a spare or two.

Greg gives us his views on why head-gaskets can fail on K-Series engines 'Wow! Where do you want to start? There are a number of causes; sticking thermostats, revving a cold engine too high, soft cylinder heads, shifting cylinder liners... there are a lot of possibles. If the head-gasket on the car has failed, it is important to establish how it failed. This is where sometimes the disproportionate bill for such work can happen. If a head has been off, a number of checks should have been carried out if the repairer is worth their salt.'

One fundamental issue is the height of the cylinder liners, which need to protrude a fraction above the bore. Greg explains: 'a head gasket failure can sometimes be missed, in that the actual failure is not due to a gasket going, it's usually due to something else, and if it's not fixed properly then it's going to happen again inevitably. What you have to check for is the protrusion in the cylinder liner – 0.06mm (0.002in) is not too bad and we would put a standard head gasket on and that would be fine. If they are flush with the head, that's when it's a problem; protruding slightly is fine. Installing new liners is a job for an engineering firm like Scholar (in UK) for example. The block would be heated, the old liners would be popped out, new ones put back in and the machining required to do that would be done in one go. It's an engine out job. What we tend to find is that when someone's faced with an big bill for a head gasket to be done and the head skimmed – if it's found that the liners are flush and there's no protrusion – then they ask us to patch her up,

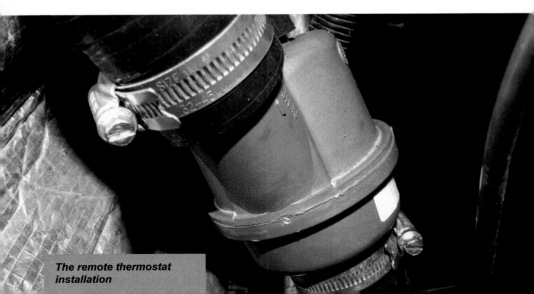

The remote thermostat installation

get her on the road and the car will be sold. That's beyond what people expect to have to do and unfortunately that has led to cars coming back in the hands of the new owner who has experienced head gasket failure and they are not happy. We try to be up front and give good advice. If the liners are replaced properly then realistically you should be able to get 60-80k miles from a K-Series engine without the gasket going. There's a lot of hysteria out there – "it misfired when I pulled it out of the garage this morning, is the head gasket going?!" – 50 percent of that is correct but the rest is hysteria. Land Rover did a big recall and they changed the position of the thermostat because the way the thermostat allows the engine to warm up allows for a cold shock from the cool air in the rad when the thermostat opens. What we use is a Rover kit which reverses the flow through the cylinder head so you don't get that shock that causes the failure sometimes.'

It seems then that the worst thing you can do is start the car up on your driveway, drive until it's just below thermostat opening point and then switch off and go into your office; but that must happen all the time. Greg's advice on warming up a K-series motor is, 'avoid going over 3000rpm for the first 20- to 25 minutes, wait for the temperature to get to 86 and then give it another 10 minutes after that to make sure everything is warmed up and working.' And you have the patience of a saint.

SUMMARY OF K-SERIES ENGINE CHECKS

Check on any bill for a head gasket change that these tests have been done.

❏ Hardness and pressure test
This ensures that the head is still serviceable and is an essential part of the head skimming. If it isn't done, you may re-assemble everything only

for the problem to happen again six months later.
❏ Cylinder liner protrusion check
While the head is off, the cylinder liners should be inspected to make sure they are still protruding above the surface of the block (it's a very small amount!) This should appear on any bill relating to the head-gasket work - otherwise there is a risk of recurrence later.

❏ Flushing of the oil and cooling system
Depending on the nature of the failure, the coolant paths and oil-ways need to be cleaned of all the gunk that can be created with head gasket failure. This should be on the bill.'

❏ Gaskets and head-bolts
The type of gasket used should depend on the vehicle's intended application, how much has been skimmed from the head and how much cylinder liner-protrusion is present. For example, you wouldn't want to use a thick multi-layer motorsport head-gasket on a car where there is very little cylinder liner protrusion present. In this instance, the most recent derivative of the Rover head-gasket would be preferable.

❏ Cooling system check
Checks that the cooling system does not have any leaks that might prevent the system reaching normal operating temperature. For example a split and cracked coolant reservoir is a common cause of head-gasket failure. They become dry and cracked, and then will not hold pressure.

❏ Routine dipstick check
This is a regular owner check. Always warm-up the car slowly and, once coolant temperature is reached, wait another 5-10 minutes for the oil temperature to catch up before placing load on the engine. Pull the dipstick frequently, when the

An alloy throttle body - it's less prone to the butterfly sticking

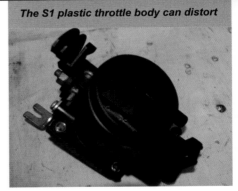

The S1 plastic throttle body can distort

car is warm after a journey and check for mayonnaise in the oil. Sometimes damage to the head can occur if a problem isn't found early enough. 'We've never had a record of oil starvation with the K-Series engine,' is Greg's experience, 'so there's never been any call to put a baffled sump in that, but the Toyota sump is a big hole waiting for oil to move around.'

THROTTLE BODY

On early Series 1 cars the accelerator could stick so the engine idled at higher than normal speeds – say, 2000rpm. It wasn't merely a feature of the automatic choke and happened long after the engine reached operating temperature. It was traceable to the throttle cable which stretched or stuck due to rain ingress or engine-bay heat at the throttle body end, and while putting another turn in the throttle return spring provided a short-term fix the extra strain could actually distort the throttle body and

the problem would recur. The factory subsequently replaced the S1's plastic throttle body with an aluminium version that was less prone to the sticking problems, and a replacement cost £80 ($120). Greg has this to say: 'the plastic throttle body is not cut out for the heat it is subjected to, and can become damaged if the induction hose is over-tightened. The net effect of the heat over time is that the throttle-body becomes very slightly misshapen and the butterfly inside sticks to the sidewall. There is a short-term fix, which we do that involves removing the throttle-body and lightly sanding the sidewalls to free up the movement of the butterfly, but this only lasts for about 5,000 miles (8,000km). The best solution is to replace it with an alloy throttle-body (as per the MG 160 throttle bodies). This is the perfect solution. The 111S has a 52mm alloy throttle-body fitted as standard.'

Another issue with the S1 accelerator is that the pivot bolt in the complex cable mechanism under the dash can work loose. Adjusting the cable will achieve partial throttle opening but if it's gone undetected for a while, chances are the bolt threads will be damaged and it will need to be replaced.

SUPERCHARGED ENGINES

As we've seen, aftermarket forced induction doesn't win Guy's vote, but interestingly, Greg has a different take on supercharging: he's much more positive, to the extent that you shouldn't necessarily dismiss a supercharged car provided it's been properly executed. 'I love the K-Series,' says Greg. 'It's probably one of the best engines – it's small and light, has good power, is easy to work on, the parts are easy to get hold of and it features in many cars. But I don't think Turbo Technics thought that people would be pushing them quite so hard.'

However, Hangar 111 offer a Turbo Technics kit, having taken over that aspect of the blower specialist's business.

'We were developing supercharger kits for the 111R and the Exige and we were getting 215bhp (158kW) reliably so I thought, why don't we re-visit the Turbo-Technics kit. We bought the lot because they didn't want to get involved with it anymore. We've changed it slightly and we can't use the Turbo Technics name on it, but they've given us their blessing to use the components.'

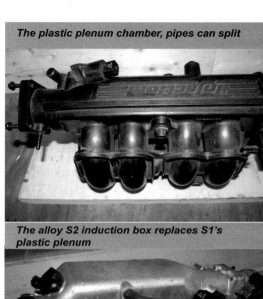

The plastic plenum chamber, pipes can split

The alloy S2 induction box replaces S1's plastic plenum

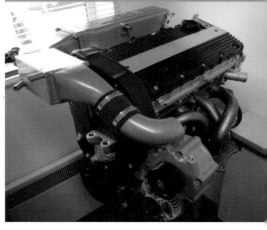

K-series twin-cam with Hangar 111's Turbo Tecnics supercharger fitted

Greg believes it's the ultimate evolution of the K-Series engine, fed by a neat Turbo Technics style compressor and plenum, perfectly mated using a bracket to rotate the alternator to provide space for a continuous belt and adjustor. 'You run a low boost and lower compression pistons and you get around 215bhp and it's completely linear and smooth. The original Turbo Technics charge cooler is far too small; it's tiny and you have a fairly small pre-cooler at the front of the car, so we've redesigned it and we're making it three times as big,' says Greg. 'We are changing other things like the secondary injectors; you don't need those if you have the right size injectors and ECU to run the engine – Emerald have the perfect ECU for the K-Series engine.' Hangar 111 offers a low-boost application that gives around 200bhp (147kW) but uses standard pistons and rods. The compression is reduced in the cylinder head and using a thicker head gasket to achieve around 0.35 bar (5psi)

boost. As Greg says, 'that's just low enough to look after the engine but enough to give you a nice smooth, torquey characteristic.'

SERIES 1 GEARBOX

Gearboxes are generally bombproof, though woes on '96/'97 cars' transmissions focus on the roll-pin in the gearshift falling out and making gear selection impossible. On the whole, shift quality differs from car to car. For example, Honda transmissions can pop out of 5th gear due to a tolerance factor, while selecting reverse is sometimes difficult because of a design fault, which also makes it moan in motion. The 111S's close-ratio 'box whines on overrun in 5th thanks to resonance generated by the gear selector mechanism, transmitted into the cockpit via the gear linkage. Lotus abandoned the solution as it made the shift less precise. The gear linkages under the rear of the car tend to wear fairly

Corrosion and oil on gear selectors

Elise 111 cockpit, with radio fitted

badly, and the short answer is to replace them.

The clutch pedal can become stiff to operate due to the need for lubrication, swiftly sorted with a squirt of WD-40 or drop of grease at the pivot point. A loose pedal on the extruded arm will produce a clicking noise, mended with 2-pack epoxy glue and a pop rivet.

ACCESSORIES

It goes without saying that you'll check that all the lights and indicators, wiper, horn and controls are in good order. Make sure you have the full control of the heater: it should be working properly on 1, 2 and 3 on the switches. There can be a rheostat problem, the electronic control for the fan; they can break down – though it's not common. Just make sure that all the buttons and lights work.

Elise Series 2

The basic checks are the same as for the Series 1, with the following points to note.

CHASSIS AND BODYWORK

Look for any untoward damage underneath the chassis areas, bending or tears. There are no floorpan corrosion issues, as S2s never had the bonded mats.

Blistering on the bodywork can be an issue, specifically on an S2 because it's materially different from the hand-laid fibreglass construction of the S1. S2 clams and panels are composed of an SMC compound made in a different process by SOTIRA in France. According to Guy, 'the areas to pay attention to are mainly along the seams of the front and rear clams where there can be a blistering fracture line or a small cluster of blistering. It's not bad workmanship, and it's not necessarily down to an accident; it's to do with the nature of the material, the SMC, where filler is applied to give a nice line. If the SMC adjoining the filled area has moved, it gives contour mapping or even a fracture which looks like a blister on a line.' Not that common, nevertheless worth a look on a 5- to 8-year old car.

WINDOW WINDERS

The window guides in the S2 window channels don't have the same issues with the felts as the S1, but there are nylon blocks on the side of the window glass itself that can wear and make for a rattling window. It's not so tight against the seal as to provide a watertight sealing on the rubbers. On later S2s the electric windows are not normally a problem, though there have been central locking issues with later cars but that's just a module matter.

BAD VIBES

The hood tensioners may rattle when the roof is off, and the handbrake cables can vibrate on the undertray. Vibrations emanating from the rear window are down to the minimal gap between the glass and the body panels and it's not unknown for the rear window to come unstuck and have to be rebonded at the factory.

DOOR KNOCKS

A few early Series 2 cars were built using smaller door striker pins, so that the doors vibrate on poor roads and potholes. There are upgrades that can be fitted, like a wider pin to take up some slack in the door catch area to stop it rattling. The striker pins can be replaced or the assembly adjusted by raising the striker by 1mm (0.04in).

FRONT ACCESS PANELS

The screen washer bottle is accessed by removing the front panel, and the screw fixings can be troublesome and require care so as not to scratch the panels or central bonnet ridge.

INTERIOR

There's inevitably going to be some wear and tear within the cabin, as Guy points out. 'On the sill (rocker) pad to the door shut it is quite common to have scuffing to its leather or keprotec trim – that's the very hard wearing rubberised plastic woven surface which is also found on the edges of the seats. These are

Lotus upholsterers are one of the company's best kept secrets. A 2010 Elise 1.6

straightforward enough to replace.' There were problems with rippling in the alcantara trim on the dash, though after May 2001 Lotus changed the adhesive to cure the issue.

If things are in a real state all is not lost. 'The Lotus upholsterers are one of their best kept secrets,' says Guy. 'Take it to Hethel and it is not expensive to have everything restored to as-new condition. On a Series 1 they had a leather sill cover which was double-sided sticky-taped on, and they can be just taken off and replaced.'

The seats can sometimes squeak, and as well as pushing the driver's seat as far forward as it'll go and greasing the runners, the likely remedy is to tighten up the Allen bolts holding the seat to the floor.

AIR CONDITIONING AND HEATING

Guy always specifies cars with air conditioning. He uses it all year round because it helps to dehumidify the car as well as keep temperature down, and he believes that it doesn't steal a significant amount of power – or rather than the small cost in oomph and weight is worth the large benefit in comfort. I'm not so sure, based on my experience of driving an Elise from the Grand Canyon to Las Vegas – it was air con or die, and I definitely felt that my car's grunt was a little subdued. When I turned it off for a blacktop blast on the old Route 66 up to Seligman the car seemed to respond with new verve. It was truer still driving one in Florida the following year, though the humidity was such I didn't care at all. However, it's not a deal breaker for Guy, particularly since many people are only looking for a recreational car for sunny days and topless motoring. The air conditioning system on the Elise isn't particularly strong because it has to be comparatively compact and lightweight, but it's fairly reliable. In terms of specifying from new, £1,000 for a complete

air con system for an Elise may not pay for itself either, since many buyers don't require it, though it is a different matter for the Exige, where you can't take the roof off.

The Elise heater fan takes care of screen misting in a very short time and being a small cockpit it doesn't take long to warm through. However there have been glitches. The cable that controls airflow from screen to footwell can require adjustment to be sure the breeze is channelled into the footwell when the lever is hard over to the left. Bizarrely, the foam packaging protecting the heater unit in transit from supplier to Hethel production line occasionally got forgotten during assembly, the result being a hail of confetti through the air vents when the fan was first operated, and there may be some residue of this left in the system.

STEERING AND SUSPENSION

There are the normal suspension areas to check, looking out for play and impact damage. Bearings are stronger on the S2 than on the S1 and there's rarely a need to change them, so any play detectable in the steering rack is likely to be down to wear and tear. Always check the UJ column that attaches directly onto the rack where there are two universal joints. Guy advises, 'if there's movement, sometimes you can get away with just a nip-up of the UJ or else it's into a rack replacement. Those sensitive racks can be damaged by impact with a pothole, and the wheels can get bent. They're delicate wheels for a delicate car, but they are certainly not frail.'

ENGINE AND GEARBOX
ENGINE NOISES

If a K-series engine seems excessively noisy at start-up, with the noise going away after a few minutes, it's most likely to be due to noisy

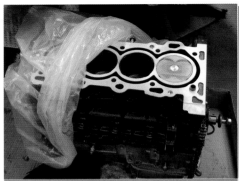

A rebuilt Toyota 1.8-litre engine awaits its cylnder head

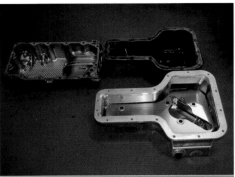

Oil pans: K-series (top right), regular Toyota (left) and aftermarket (front)

tappets, which in extreme circumstances will require attention. Toyota engines appear to be problem free – until they're subjected to trackday use. It's not just a missed downshift that can bounce the revs to oblivion. As owners become more familiar with the Elise's on-track handling abilities, maybe further enhanced with uprated suspension packages, the cars are subjected to consistently higher cornering forces over longer periods. This leads to oil starvation – and the engines suffer accordingly. Greg explains: 'when the Elise and Exige came out with more power, people started to take them very seriously as trackday and race cars. They already did with the K-Series engines, of course, but more people now saw the opportunity because the Toyota engine was perceived as a lot more robust and durable. But what we've found is that the guys with the Toyota engine are pushing the cars beyond their limit, and finding out after 20 or 30 track days that durability is becoming an issue. And during that time their technique behind the wheel is getting better and better and they're competent to push the car even harder.'

There's no rev limiter so if you go from 5th to 2nd at 6000rpm the engine is going to go way beyond its 8000rpm limit. 'This is one of the issues with an engine that develops most of its torque at high revs; tolerance has to be spot on. The engine was developed by Yamaha originally so it's designed to take that sort of abuse,' Greg admits, 'but it's not designed to take that sort of abuse in the conditions that it's being put through in the Elise and the Exige. A lot of it comes down to G-force,' he says. 'If you've put semi-slick tyres on the car it's going to generate plenty more lateral G than, say, the Celica it was designed for, but in the back of the car where there's lots of grip, pulling plenty of Gs, and the oil-slop is the only thing that's going to give. We've got solutions: the main thing is to fit a baffled sump to the car as it solves the problem before it happens.

We recommend and fit Moroso baffled oil pans; they make some of the coolest, top quality stuff, and from drag racing they know all about oil movement and what to do about it. We've worked with them to perfect the oil pan and we've sold hundreds. The essence of it is the internal flanges (baffles) that control and manage the inertia of the oil, plus it holds almost an extra litre of oil. A side effect is that it's made of aluminium, it's a thinner material and therefore the heat transfer is greater, so it provides a cooling effect over and above that of the original. It's one of our best selling products. Some people prefer the Accusump, which manages the oil pressure, so if there's a detected drop in the engine oil pressure more oil is added until the engine oil pressure comes up to what it should be and then that oil is taken away. That deals with the problem when it's already happened, but by the time you've had low oil pressure then the oil pump is going to have had some issues. A combination of the baffled and Accusump is the ideal solution.'

A blown engine isn't entirely a catastrophe, as new blocks for the Toyota 1.8 engine are readily available: 'Toyota have a good stock, even though Lotus have kissed it goodbye. The engines are very common in the US, but Toyota in the UK can provide new blueprinted blocks that are exceptional quality. We can do the cylinder head repairs, we out-source those to Scholar Engines, whom we've used for years. They fit uprated stainless steel valves too.' Greg recalls some Toyota horrors: 'we had one with the piston on number 4 cylinder chewed to pieces. A valve was twisted sideways and wedged into the head. You think, wow, that's never going to be repairable, but they are, and they come back fully pressure tested and you don't have to hardness check them because they are exceptional quality.'

GEAR LINKAGE
If the 2nd gearshift action on an S2 is balky it

Corroded earth terminal onto the chassis

could be that the gear linkage is awry. It shouldn't be difficult to move from any gear to another, though the movement is always smoother if it's not rushed. It's important not to force the lever through the gate, as the balking will just get worse.

NON-STARTER

Starting problems can simply be due to corroded terminals on the starter motor. If nothing happens when the ignition key is turned, except for the Stack unit lights glowing and the fuel pump whirring, it could be the starter motor terminals or worn brushes, calling for a new or reconditioned unit.

RESTORED CARS

Greg's Hangar 111 business is experiencing a demand for 'brand new' Elise Series 1s: 'a lot of people ask us to provide them with the parts to make their Elise brand new again – apart from the chassis, though that can be done. Normally we sell them the parts and equipment to make the car better than it was originally from a durability point of view. But we have totally renovated several cars to as-new condition and now the Exige guys are coming out of the wood-work and they are asking us to re-build their Toyota cars to make them like new again – and they are not even that old!' As prospective purchases go, such cars are very attractive because the seller or previous owner has already made the heavy investment. Whilst a restored car is a more attractive proposition than one that's not, the expenses incurred are never fully reflected in its market value. Crucially, if contemplating a restored or extensively refurbished car, you need to be sure the work has been carried out, invoiced and documented photographically by an acknowledged Lotus expert using first-rate componentry.

IN SUMMARY

So, there are plenty of things to think about before splashing the cash. The experts we've consulted here – one a franchised dealer, the other an independent specialist – represent both sides of the Lotus fraternity on Elises in particular, so both have vested interests in making sure the best cars remain in play. Their advice and the points they raise are well worth investigating when viewing and trying prospective cars.

The golden rule when buying any car is that if there is something you feel is 'not right' – even if you cannot put your finger on it – walk away. But if you take on board the advice given here, you'll be better placed to make value judgements about the prospective purchase. Make a checklist of bullet points from their observations and make sure all the boxes can be ticked as you work your way around the car. That way you'll avoid trouble, or worse, buying a pup.

Take a friend or, better still, a Lotus expert with you. We would suggest you look at – and drive – several cars to get a range of experiences to weigh up their attributes and so allowing you to make a more informed choice.

If your country has a requirement for an annual roadworthiness check, for peace of mind at the outset you'll no doubt be wanting a car with a new or recent test certificate. In the UK, this is the annual VoSA (MoT) check and you should ask to see all the related paperwork, which includes the list of 'advisories' – suggestions and recommendations from the test station about what may want doing in the near future. That will give you an independent general appraisal about its general condition as well as a heads-up as to whether there are any big bills in the offing.

Elise S2 and the author on the road to Montserrat (near Barcelona, Spain)

The Vehicle Identification Number (VIN) is normally located in three places:
On a sticker on the inside of the windscreen.

On a sticker in the front services compartment.

Stamped vertically on the chassis, approximately level with the front of the rear offside wheel.

What do the letters and numerals signify? From the Elise service notes for 1996 and 1997 model, here's how to interpret them:

SCC in position 123 is manufacturer's code
111 in position 456 is Elise
YN1 in position 789 is Engine type of 1.8 K16
Model year is position 10
T=96
V=97
W=98
X=99
Y=2000
1=2001, 2=2002, etc
H in position 11 is plant (Hethel)

A in position 12 means right-hand drive
F in position 12 means left-hand drive
Engine emission spec is position 13
Model number is position 14, eg Elise
Serial number is 15, 16 and 17

From 1998, the Elise service notes identify:
SCC in pos 123 is the manufacturer code
G in position 4 is the standard 1.8 K-series engine, J means it's the VVC version
A in position 5 is Restraint (Active belts)
111 in position 678 is Elise
Position 9 is check digit
Position 10 is Model year
W=98
X=99
Y=2000
Position 11 indicates plant: H=Hethel, B=Shah Alam, Malaysia
C in position 12 is for RHD
D in position 12 is for LHD
3 in position 13 is the model, eg Elise
8 in position 13 is for the Exige
14,15,16,17 is the serial number

SPECIALISTS United Kingdom

GUY MUNDAY
STRATTON MOTOR
COMPANY
Lotus Sales Manager
Ipswich Road
Long Stratton
Norfolk, NR15 2XJ
Tel: +44 1508 530491
Fax: +44 1508 531670

M: +44 7718 385168
E: lotussales@
strattonmotorcompany.com
www.strattonmotor
company.com

GREG LOCK
HANGAR 111 LOTUS
PERFORMANCE
Unit 8b, Seven Acres Bus. Park
Newbourne Road
Waldringfield
Woodbridge, Suffolk, IP12 4PS
Tel: +44 (0)1473 811 811
www.hangar111.com

PAT THOMAS KELVEDON LOTUS
Bourne Road
Spalding
Lincolnshire
PE11 3ND
Tel: +44 (0)1775 725 457
Fax: +44 (0)1775 710 199
E: lotusguru@kelsport.net

PAUL MATTY SPORTS CARS LTD
12 Old Birmingham Road,
Bromsgrove,
Worcestershire,
B60 1DE.
Tel: +44 (0)1527 835 656
Fax: +44 (0)1527 575172
E: enquiries@paulmattysports
cars.co.uk.

BARRY ELY SPORTS CARS
453 High Road,
Leyton,
London, E10 5EL.
Tel: +44 20 8558 3221
Mob: +44 7836 206 790
Fax: +44 20 8539 9500
E: lotuscarsales@aol.com
www.barryelysportscars.co.uk

STEVE WILLIAMS SPORTS CARS
5 Cordwallis Street,
Maidenhead,
Berkshire, SL6 7BE
Tel: +44 1628 770066
E: info@swlotus.com
www.swlotus.com

SJ SPORTSCARS LTD
Independent Lotus Specialists
Unit 1 Ash Down End
Lords Meadow Industrial Estate
Crediton,
Devon EX17 1HN
Tel / Fax: +441363 777790
E: steve@sjsportscars.co.uk
www.sjsportscars.co.uk

ALLON WHITE SPORTS CARS
119 High Street
Cranfield
Bedfordshire
MK43 0BS
Tel: 0844 573 1966
Fax: 0845 345 7695
Tel (from abroad): +44
1234 750205
E: sales@allonwhite.co.uk
www.allonwhite.co.uk

PAUL CLUGSTON UK SPORTSCARS
Wingham Engineering Estate
Wingham
Canterbury, Kent
Tel: +44 1227 728190
E: sales@uksportscars.com
www.uksportscars.com

PURE LOTUS LTD
1 Moat House Square
Thorpe Arch Trading Estate
Wetherby
Yorkshire, LS23 7BJ
Tel: +44 1937 844633
Mob: +44 7816 822319
FAX: +44 1937 844633
www.purelotus.co.uk

WAYNE SWEETING ESSEX AUTOSPORT
Sinclaire House
Bryant Avenue
Gallows Corner
Romford, RM3 0AP
www.essexautosport.com
Tel: + 44 1708 343904
Fax:+44 1708 381187
E: wayne@essexautosport.
com (bodyshop & tuning
enquiries)

COMPREHENSIVE DEDICATED WEBSITE
www.elises.co.uk

ELISEPARTS.COM LTD,
Unit 6 Lotus Court,
Harvard Way,
Harvard Industrial Estate,
Kimbolton, Cambridgeshire,
PE28 0LS
Tel: 0845 226 1012
Fax: +44 1480 869168
International Tel: + 44
1480 860002
www.eliseparts.com

ELISE/EXIGE HONDA ENGINE CONVERSION:
www.hondaelise.com
www.stark-automotive.co.uk

JOHNNY TIPLER

Johnny Tipler is a freelance motoring journalist and author, with 35 books published on a variety of topics ranging from car and motorcycle production to racing driver biographies. His tally includes eight books on Lotus models alone, including the Types 25 and 33, 78 and 79 single-seater Formula 1 cars and, most recently, the Lotus Evora. A great fan of the marque, Johnny writes regularly for the in-house Lotus Club International magazine, penning drive stories and interviews. He also specialises in Porsche topics, and frequently covers historic race meetings such as Goodwood Revival, Spa Six Hours and La Carrera Panamericana for the classic motoring media worldwide.

Johnny is married with four children and lives in Norwich, Norfolk, and also has a home in the Douro region of northern Portugal, where the roads that twist around the hillsides are tailor-made for the Elise. See his website at www.johntipler.co.uk.

Acknowledgements

This has been a treat to research and write and I'm especially grateful to everyone who's provided tips and information about the Elise and what to look for when shopping for one. In particular I want to mention Guy Munday of Stratton Motor Company, Greg and Marianne Lock of Hangar 111 and Matt Becker, ride and handling guru at Lotus Cars.

The majority of photographs were provided by Lotus Cars' archives, for which thanks to Alastair Florance, John Lamb and Tracey Parnell. In-house snapper Jason Parnell/Lotus Cars provided the stunning cover image and furnished me with shots from some of our drive trips. Thanks to Lotus Club International editor Caroline Parker for allowing us to reproduce them. Thanks are also due to photographers Antony Fraser and Wim te Riet.

ULTIMATE BUYERS GUIDES INCLUDE:

■ Porsche 911SC 1977 to 1983;
ISBN 0 9545579 0 5

■ Porsche 911 Carrera (964) 1989 to 1994;
ISBN 978 0 954999 04 9

■ Porsche 911 Carrera (993) 1993 to 1998;
ISBN 978 0 954999 01 8

■ Porsche 944 and 968 (1981-1995);
ISBN 978 1 906712 07 5

■ Porsche Boxster & Cayman 1996 to 2007;
ISBN 978 0 954999 06 3

■ Porsche 911 (996) All models inc Turbo & GT;
ISBN 978 0 954999 07 0

■ Porsche 911 (997) All models incl Turbo and GT 2004-2009; ISBN 978 1 906712 00 6

■ Porsche 911 The Classic Models (1964-1989) inc Turbo & 912; ISBN 978 0 954999 09 4

■ MGF and TF; ISBN 0 9545579 6 4

■ Land Rover Discovery; ISBN 0 9545579 7 2

■ Porsche 944 & 968; ISBN 978 0 954557 99 7

■ Subaru Impreza; ISBN 0 9545579 8 0

■ Honda CBR900 and CBR1000 (FireBlade);
ISBN 978 0 954999 03 2

■ Lotus Elise in all its forms (incl Exige & Europa) 1995-2011; ISBN 978 1 906712 09 9

ULTIMATE OWNERS' GUIDES INCLUDE:

■ Porsche 911 Carrera 3.2; ISBN 978 1 906712 02 0

■ Porsche 911 Carrera (993);
ISBN 978 1 906712 06 8

■ Porsche Boxster & Cayman;
ISBN 978 1 906712 01 3

■ Porsche 911 (996) in all its forms;
ISBN 978 1 906712 03 7